AF720039

"What a concept: Structure a process for Producers and Consumers of information necessary for a successful integration to collaborate directly and efficiently without unnecessary noise and hierarchy. What comes across clearly is that Cris Casey curated the CRISP concepts through extensive experience deep in the integration trenches. These are valuable lessons."

Michael L. Weiner, Steptoe LLP

* * * * *

"Your methodology offers a robust framework for streamlining M&A execution, and I commend the clarity and structure of your approach. I believe CRISP has the potential to significantly improve the efficiency and effectiveness of M&A initiatives."

Claudia Dochow, Founder in Chief, Chief Operations Ltd., plus
Founder & Business Angel, Canitoga Foundation

* * * * *

"The content is very to the point, thorough, accurate and appropriate. Mr. Casey shares his unusual insight into complex organizations undergoing radical system change and somehow manages to transform this task into a tasty snack."

Dr. R. Mosely, PhD., General Manager Corion (retired)

* * * * *

"The subject matter of M & A can easily feel heavy for first timers, but you manage to give it momentum and to me at least it felt like reading a novel with a storyline. Sharper in focus and more welcoming for a reader who may not yet be immersed in the world of M&A execution. I particularly like the clarity in which you have articulated the main (or core) issue i.e. <It's not strategy—it's execution. Specifically: communication, coordination, and timely delivery.>"

Mr. Bhushan Malik (London, UK)

"The author nails a painful truth: poor execution and constant reporting cycles cripple progress. This book delivers a refreshing, actionable framework that tackles the issue head-on. Your vision can be shiny, your goal noble, but if you lack execution, you won't get anywhere."

Agnese Jaunosane, co-founder at Ajelix

* * * * *

"First off, this isn't a book, it's a blueprint. You call it a "field-hardened structure" and you're not kidding. I mean, this thing is dense, in a good way. It's not a casual read. You've written a serious manual for a very specific person, someone in the trenches with a painful, expensive problem on their hands.

What I really like is that you're not writing another high-level book on M&A strategy. You're tackling the actual execution hell: the "endless meetings, duplicate reporting, unclear accountability, and constant interruptions". The whole thing is built to cut out noise, and you hit that point hard.

The best part, for me, is the Key Artifacts. You don't just talk theory; you give them the literal tools. The NPX, the Colleague Roster, the Employee Matrix, all of it. You're handing them actionable templates. And making it tech-agnostic? That's a brilliant move. Stating right out that it works in their existing tools just lowers the barrier to entry. It feels practical, not like a sales pitch for a new platform.

I also appreciate that you included the "why" in the appendices. Grounding the system in communication theory and neuroscience gives it a ton of credibility. It shows exactly why the old ways, like trying to force-fit Agile or Waterfall, just don't work for this.

So, will readers like it?

Here's the breakdown. A casual business reader? No. They will be completely lost by page 15.

But the right reader? "Like" isn't the right word. They will value it immensely.

Your target audience, those corporate development leaders, IMO/PMO heads, and consultants, doesn't need another inspirational story. They need a system that works.

This book is a tool. No one's going to "like" it the way they like a story, right? But they will love it because it's an actionable solution to a problem that's probably given them sleepless nights and cost their company a fortune.

I also really appreciate your honesty about where it won't work. Calling out "rigid, hierarchical organizations" and cultures with "low levels of trust" is a critical, honest-to-god disclaimer.

My final take? It's a fantastic reference and manual. You've codified a massive amount of experience. It's not a light read, but for the people in the M&A trenches, it's exactly the kind of practical, no-fluff playbook they've been looking for."

Pradeep Sanyal, Capgemini Senior Technologist and Advisor

* * * * *

"What stood out to me is how effectively CRISP captures the operational reality of M&A. It offers a clear, field-tested system for surfacing deliverables, aligning cross-functional teams, and reducing the friction that slows integrations down. The concepts are practical, grounded, and highly usable for anyone responsible for making deal execution work.

The tone is confident and authoritative, which fits the purpose of the book. The detailed style reinforces that CRISP is a real system and not a theoretical model. Each concept gets enough space to be fully explained. It feels like a field manual from someone who has truly done this work."

Klint Kendrick, PhD., SPHR, CEO HR M&A Roundtable

* * * * *

"The model could be the new contemporary method for efficient program management. I also think the framework could be applied to many corporate process change programs beyond just M&A."

Major PMI thought leader and contributor (name withheld by request)

Optimizing M&A Execution with CRISP™

Mitigating the Risk of
Using Yesterday's Playbooks
in Today's World

Cris Casey

Optimizing M&A Execution with CRISP™ Copyright © 2026 by Cris Casey.

All rights reserved. No part of this publication may be reproduced, distributed or transmitted in any form or by any means, including photocopying, recording, or other electronic or mechanical methods, without the prior written permission of the publisher, except in the case of brief quotations embodied in critical reviews and certain other noncommercial uses permitted by copyright law.

All trademarks belong to their respective owners.

Although the author and publisher have made every effort to ensure that the information in this book was correct at press time, the author and publisher do not assume and hereby disclaim any liability to any party for any loss, damage, or disruption caused by errors or omissions, whether such errors or omissions result from negligence, accident, or any other cause.

Disclaimer: This book is designed to provide general information for our readers. It is sold with the understanding that the publisher is not engaged to render any type of legal, business or any other kind of professional advice. The content of this book is the sole expression and opinion of the author, and not necessarily that of the publisher. No warranties or guarantees are expressed or implied by the author's choice to include any of the content in this book. Neither the publisher nor the author shall be liable for any physical, psychological, emotional, financial, or commercial damages, including, but not limited to, special, incidental, consequential or other damages. The reader is responsible for their own choices, actions, and results.

Optimizing M&A Execution with CRISP™ / Casey, Cris. - 1st ed.

Published by Prominence Publishing.

ISBN: 978-1-997649-28-1

CONTENTS

PREFACE

The experiences that led to writing this book are based on a lifetime of interaction with talented and insightful people. While there are not enough pages to mention everyone who influenced me, here is an attempt to recognize some of them.

Who to thank first is always a challenge. but I think I am safe in starting with those individuals who had the courage (and insight) to engage me for some of their most challenging initiatives. So I start with Ron Cardone, who, over roughly 30 years, engaged me to help with critical initiatives he encountered with each new company he worked for. Other clients who used my services multiple times, and who I now consider personal friends include Beverly Tyler, Doug Skillins, Stein Tumert, and Jon Marks. It is not an overstatement to say that without their support this book would not have been possible.

Next, the value of having outside voices weigh-in on early manuscripts is immeasurable. So I can't express enough gratitude to my advanced readers: David W. Power, Michael Weiner, Pradeep Sanyal, David Mantica, Bhushan Malik, Ron Cardone, Jon Marks, and Agnese Jaunosane for their valuable editorial and experiential feedback.

The CRISP™ marketing and delivery websites are critical components of getting the word out and April Mazac (The Perky Pixel) in LaGrange, Texas has been handling my WordPress admin and layout needs for over 10 years. So too is on-going LinkedIn and database/email handling work performed by Larissa Dy in the Philippines who has been a trusted resource for as long as April.

Experience directing the production of books for clients early in the Marcomm phase of my career made me acutely aware of the process and criticality of the team. Here is the outstanding international team involved for this effort: chapter heading art was created by Uros Pajic in Serbia, copy editing by Jason Findlay in South Africa, typesetting and layout by Heather Mize in the US, book cover design by Nanjar Tri Mukti in Indonesia. and of course my publisher Suzanne Doyle-Ingram (Prominence Publishing) in Vancouver, Canada for handling the administrative and creative orchestration, initial promotion, and providing nuanced publishing advice.

My career would not be what it is without the moral support and encouragement, some going back 50+ years, from the likes of Scott Carlin, Ken Diamond, Jim Kann, Hank Birkdale, Jack Dettis, Christine Kiezulas, and Marc Burns.

And last but not least I want to thank my wife, Rebecca Gray-Casey, who, over 30 years ago listening to modem handshake tones before connecting to an AOL chatroom, took a huge leap of faith and chose to make a new life with me despite my somewhat non-traditional approach to generating income. I remain eternally grateful.

Introduction

While my mother gave me the confidence that I could accomplish anything I set my mind to, I can trace the initial trajectory of my career to another woman: Virginia 'Ginny' Madden-Shepard. Ginny was responsible for running a newly donated CCTV studio, installed at my school, Riverbank Elementary in Stamford, CT.

The video equipment, ancient black and white orthicon cameras with 4 lens turrets on wooden tripods, and their NASA-style circa 1960 control consoles came from Dr. Peter Goldmark, inventor of the long-playing vinyl record, and back then, president of CBS Laboratories. His granddaughter attended Riverbank.

Ginny taught me (and my best friend at the time, Scott Carlin, later to be a senior Warner Brothers executive and eventually president of HBO Domestic Distribution) how to produce live TV. We did fairy tale shows for 1st graders, map skills and geography for 3rd graders, and current events shows for 6th graders. By participating in all the roles required to create multiple live performances using communication technology and understanding the importance of orchestration of those roles, I was introduced to managing complicated projects with serious time constraints at the age of 12.

And as each year passed I found myself in the middle of complex undertakings in need of the skills I was honing along the way. 10 years later that meant traveling the world as an industrial show business technical director, staging and producing live shows for Fortune 500 clients. 20 years later after adding bespoke software application development for small business clients to my skill set, I transitioned into working with bigger and bigger businesses on bigger and more expensive engagements eventually as a pure program/project manager.

When I look back over nearly five decades spent helping companies execute their complex initiatives, about half of which dealt with mergers, acquisitions, carve-outs, spin-offs, and divestitures, I see a pattern that repeats itself almost every time. Deals are negotiated, celebrated, and signed with excitement. But as soon as execution begins, the optimism quickly gives way to frustration. Deadlines slip, budgets inflate, and the people involved find themselves mired in endless meetings, duplicate reporting, unclear accountability, and constant interruptions.

Here's a quick story with a happy ending: a $4B medical device company with 5 operating units acquired at different times was in the throes of upgrading their name-brand ERP system and adding additional functionality. Finance selected the system integrator (SI) and negotiated the deal over the objections of IT. I was injected into the initiative by the corporate controller after the 2nd, table-top, go-live attempt failed. My first question was "who is doing the testing?". The SI correctly and contractually answered the client was responsible and when given the direction to proceed, assumed testing had already been performed. My client, unaccustomed to the ways of external integrators, assumed all that "would be taken care of." Ooops.

Once this 'misunderstanding' was resolved, the effort required to design an approach to test 5 unit's new configurations, 2 new modules, and complicated accounting transactions spanning 65 countries, while the CEO tapped her foot counting down to the next quarter, could begin.

If you've been part of initiatives like this, chances are you already know this kind of pain or something like it. Transactions that look strong on paper fall apart, not because the strategy was wrong, but because the execution stumbled. Research confirms what experience makes obvious: Year after year, the majority of M&A initiatives fail to meet expectations. The root cause is rarely the big strategic questions. More often, it's the small, day-to-day breakdowns in communication, coordination, and delivery that snowball into costly overruns and preventable delays.

That is the problem this book sets out to solve.

Establishing a Connection

The material in this book is largely the result of experience gleaned from hundreds of clients who had faith that I could deliver value to their organizations. Those organizations represent a number of different industries:

- apparel
- architecture and engineering
- clinical research
- construction
- consumer products
- financial services
- food and beverages
- information technology
- medical technology
- printing technology and services
- public utilities
- semiconductor manufacturing
- telecommunications

Some firms were very large (Fortune 15) and some, not so big ($5M to $4B).

For a semi-complete picture (decades of projects take far too much space to list here), check out my project listing on LinkedIn and client comments on my personal website.

https://www.linkedin.com/in/criscasey/

https://criscasey.com/?cm_id=omae

The point of all this is this: My perspective comes not from sitting at a distance in advisory or academic chairs, but from being embedded directly in initiatives, working head-to-head alongside executives, functional leaders, and subject matter experts (SMEs), and supporting those whose efforts ultimately determine final outcomes. From this intimate position, I've seen some projects saved by small, decisive changes, while others collapsed under the weight of indecision and inefficiency.

Along the way, one truth emerged as inescapable: Execution succeeds or fails based on whether individuals—real people with names, jobs, and limited bandwidth—get the information they need, when they need it, to produce the deliverables others are counting on. Everything else is noise.

This book is written for the people who live in that noise: corporate development leaders, integration management offices, functional Workstream heads, and the advisors who support them. If you've ever asked yourself, ***"Why do we keep struggling with the same execution issues, even though we know better?"*** then this book is for you.

The Cost of Getting It Wrong

M&A volume and criticality are at all-time highs, and the percentage of enterprise transactions failing to meet expectations consistently ranges from 30-60%. Put another way, less than half of all initiatives are successful.

The economic scale of the problem is enormous.

In a 2023 study, Boston Consulting Group estimated that between 2010 and 2022, the median value of corporate divestiture deals worldwide topped $900 billion **annually**. Even applying conservative failure rates, the cost of poor post-transaction execution runs into the hundreds of **billions** of dollars **every year**.

Total failed M&A transactions represent over $450B, per year

Execution-caused failures represent over $225B, per year

While executive hubris, faulty strategic assumptions, and lack of thorough due diligence contribute significantly to absolute failures, delayed and over-budget tactical execution of integrations, which can dramatically increase transaction costs, remains a continuing source of dissatisfaction.

Behind those numbers are people. Employees, pulled away from their day jobs to answer endless requests. Leaders, burned out by the constant drag of status reporting. Buyers and sellers, watching value leak away in slow, painful increments.

The tragedy is that most of this loss is preventable.

Whether it is the exchange of documents like an employee list or single data items like a tax ID number or an executive decision, each initiative has unique constellations of transitioning elements. And, without exception, these elements have cross-functional and cross-entity (CF/CE) implications that, if properly exposed and choreographed, can accelerate the speed and precision of the integration. Or, as is often the case, if they are unnecessarily hidden and improperly managed, they can quickly retard progress and rapidly increase costs.

The data needed for execution already exists inside the organizations. The processes that use that data are well understood. The challenge is creating a structure that surfaces what matters, cuts through the noise, and gets deliverables into the right hands without delay.

What Is CRISP™?

CRISP™ is an acronym for *Colleague Responsibility Information System & Protocols,* a field-hardened structure designed to ensure execution success.

At its core, the goals of CRISP™ are simple:

- Focus only on deliverables that traverse functional or organizational boundaries.
- Make clear who is responsible for producing each deliverable and, just as important, all who will consume it.
- Establish when and how those items will be delivered, and provide access to them in a single, transparent system.
- Remove all non-essential reporting, status meetings, messaging (email and direct), and administrative overhead.

Instead of drowning contributors in tasks, CRISP™ orients them around what really matters: the timely exchange of mission-critical information. By standardizing this exchange, CRISP™ reduces noise, eliminates duplication, and creates accountability without bureaucracy.

The result is faster execution, higher-quality outcomes, and dramatically lower costs.

Before we start looking at the details, here is a graphic depiction of the major CRISP™ components:

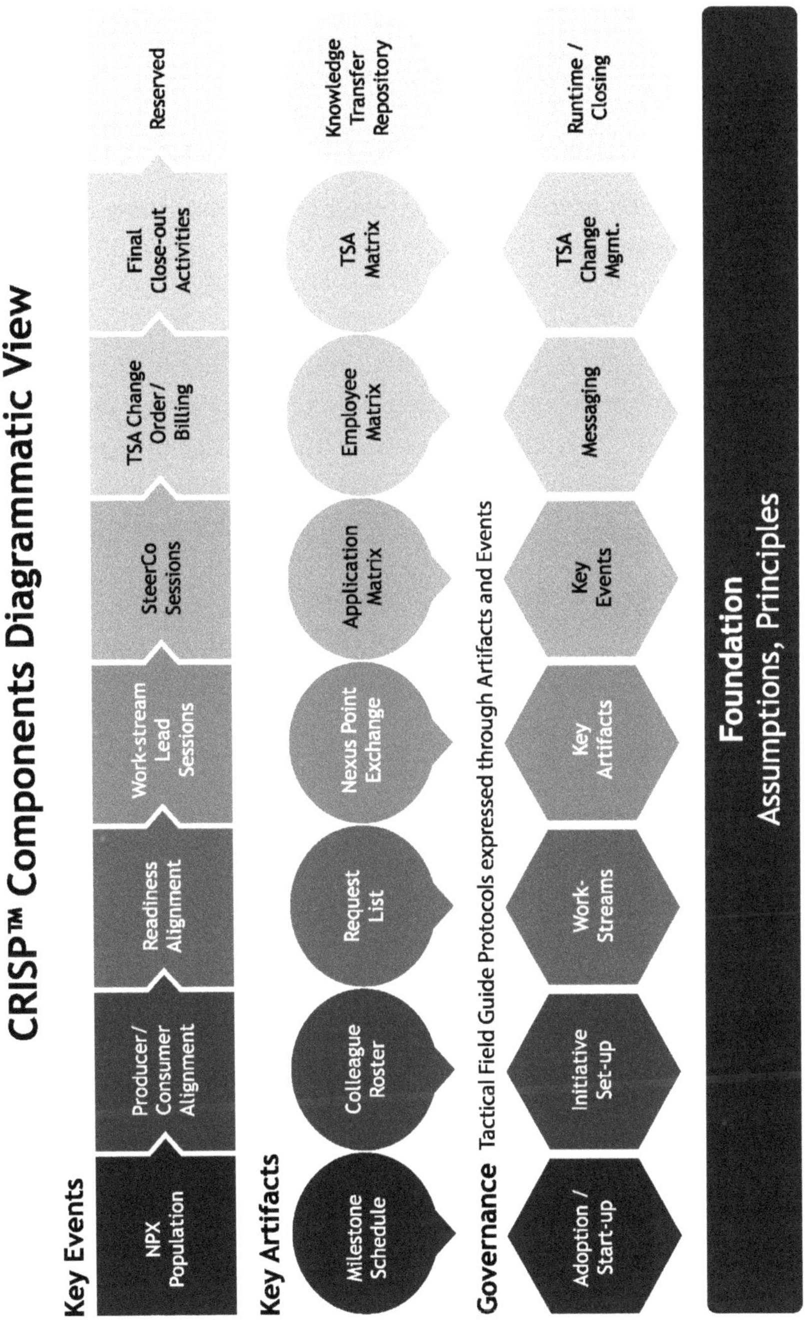
CRISP™ Components Diagrammatic View
Key Events
NPX Population
Producer/ Consumer Alignment
Readiness Alignment
Work-stream Lead Sessions
SteerCo Sessions
TSA Change Order/ Billing
Final Close-out Activities
Reserved
Key Artifacts
Milestone Schedule
Colleague Roster
Request List
Nexus Point Exchange
Application Matrix
Employee Matrix
TSA Matrix
Knowledge Transfer Repository
Governance
Tactical Field Guide Protocols expressed through Artifacts and Events
Adoption / Start-up
Initiative Set-up
Work-Streams
Key Artifacts
Key Events
Messaging
TSA Change Mgmt.
Runtime / Closing
Foundation
Assumptions, Principles

Why This Book

This book exists to do two things:

1. Show you the underlying logic and science that make CRISP™ work.
2. Provide the practical guidance you need to implement it in your own initiatives.

Others have written volumes on the financial, legal, and cultural aspects of deals. You will not find yet another discussion about how to create M&A strategy here or the necessary components of due diligence exercises. CRISP™ does not replace those efforts; it complements them. Whatever the shape of your deal, CRISP™ provides the operational backbone that ensures execution does not become the weak link.

What We Will Cover

The chapters ahead are structured to move from foundation to practice:

1. Foundation

We begin by exploring the core concepts that underpin CRISP™. You will see why traditional methods, such as Agile or Waterfall, while powerful in other contexts, break down in M&A execution. We will look at how information theory and neuroscience explain why contributors struggle under constant interruption and how CRISP™ is designed to protect attention and reduce noise. The chapter ends with a discussion of risk, and how CRISP™ addresses each risk category, or not.

2. Governance

Execution depends on clear structures. This section explains how CRISP™ defines work streams, roles, and steering committees, not as administrative overhead, but as lean mechanisms for escalation and alignment. You will see how accountability flows directly between Producer and Consumer, avoiding the bottlenecks of hierarchical filtering.

3. Key Artifacts

Artifacts are the tangible outputs that anchor CRISP™. While initiatives can have thousands of related documents, CRISP™ uses a lean set of documents to achieve its efficiency and efficacy. We will examine the Nexus Point Exchange (NPX), Colleague Roster, Employee Matrix, Application Matrix, Request List, Milestone Chart, Transition Service Agreement (TSA) Matrix, and Knowledge Transfer Repository (KTR). Each serves as a single source of truth, reducing duplication and confusion. Together, they form a strong, optimized backbone to support any initiative, regardless of size.

4. Key Events

Every initiative moves through predictable phases: Preparation, Execution and Transition. CRISP™ compresses and clarifies these phases, replacing a myriad of repetitive and non-productive status meetings with a limited number of structured alignment and readiness sessions. We will look at how to stage these events for maximum impact with minimal effort and time. This chapter also includes explanations on how to handle transition services, knowledge transfer, and close-out in ways that protect value and set the stage for future success.

5. Implementation

Last, we turn to how CRISP™ is introduced and adopted. Whether you are building a new integration management office, working within an existing one, or operating without one at all, the guidance here will show you how to embed CRISP™ protocols without disrupting what already works. We will also address confidentiality, security, and the role of technology. And last, a discussion on how CRISP™ is built to scale regardless of an initiative's type, size, or scope.

A Word of Caution

CRISP™ is not for every environment. Rigid, hierarchical organizations that rely heavily on command-and-control structures may thwart its simplicity. Cultures with low levels of trust or transparency will struggle. And those unwilling to let go of heavy Agile, Waterfall, or ingrained governance at the enterprise level may find adoption (and compliance) difficult.

But where there is a willingness to focus on people, deliverables, and communication, CRISP™ unlocks remarkable improvements. And the more often it is used, the faster, cheaper, and more predictable execution from inception to final transition becomes.

To see if your organization can take advantage of what CRISP™ offers, there is a free, initial viability analysis and recommendation service available. It's less than a dozen questions and will give you an accurate assessment of your chances for success.

https://crispmethod.com/service/ivar/?cm_id=omae

What You Can Expect

As you work through this book (some of it is admittedly dense), expect clarity. Each section is designed to be direct and practical with limited storytelling. As you've seen jargon, acronyms and abbreviations, necessary attributes of any intentionally designed system, are defined the first couple of times they are used, and also included in the Lexicon in the Appendix for ready reference. Think of it as a guidebook: concise where it can be, detailed where it must be.

If you take away only one idea, let it be this: **Execution succeeds when contributors get exactly what they need, when (or before) they need it.** That is the essence of CRISP™, and it is the lens through which every chapter is written.

Accessing High-Resolution Images and Supplemental Media

Throughout this book, select diagrams, documents, forms, and audiovisual artifacts are accessible only by QR codes or URLs. Why?

Printed pages impose limits on size, color depth, and resolution. In those cases where the full-resolution version would not be rendered properly in print, scanning the QR code, or typing the associated URL into a browser, provides access to:

- Downloadable PDFs of complex visuals and Key Artifacts
- Expanded tables and reference documents
- Supplemental explanatory videos

All linked content is controlled and maintained to ensure accuracy and continuity with the printed material.

NOTES

Foundation

A system is only as good as the foundation on which it is based. CRISP™'s foundation includes a few specialized terms, some easily understood concepts and logic, and a set of critical assumptions.

Underlying Concept

Regardless of the size, complexity, or nature of the deal, or the planning or administrative and managerial techniques used to move the initiative along, the bedrock foundation of successfully executing an enterprise-to-enterprise M&A transaction reduces to a single concept:

timely exchange of mission-critical information

The exchange is performed by subject-matter experts (SMEs) on all sides of the initiative: Buyer, Seller, Advisors/Suppliers. You already know this: Without meaningful data and information exchange, nothing happens.

WHAT'S IN A NAME?

Mentioned previously but worth repeating, CRISP™ stands for **Colleague Responsibility Information System and Protocols**. Its singular design goal is to facilitate and optimize the timely exchange of mission-critical information between all functions and entities. When the Protocols are followed using the corresponding Key Artifacts and Events, the result is an optimized method that delivers what people need, when they need it, with minimal noise and administrative friction.

Let's break down what each part of CRISP™ means:

- **Colleague.** Instead of the broad term "stakeholders," CRISP™ focuses on the people who actually make the deal happen. Whether it's a CEO making go or no-go calls, an HR analyst aligning benefits, or an IT expert managing systems, Colleagues are the ones responsible for execution.

- **Responsibility.** Every Colleague has a defined role as a Consumer and/or a Producer of information. CRISP™ Protocols and Key Artifacts ensure that everyone knows what they need to deliver, or what they need to consume, to keep the deal moving.

- **Information System.** CRISP™ isn't software; it's a structured way of managing the critical data housed in Key Artifacts. Each Artifact is derived from an optimized schema designed to support execution, ensuring that the right information gets to the right people at the right time.

- **Protocols.** These are the rules of engagement. CRISP™ provides clear behavioral guidelines, execution standards, and best practices that Colleagues follow to keep Cross Functional/Cross Entity (CF/CE) information flowing efficiently.

Base Assumptions

Assumptions are a critical element of any initiative. Some can be consequential, like assuming a market will emerge if the right product is designed, or trivial, like team parties with food will be held every Friday. CRISP™'s design is based on the following foundational assumptions derived from decades of direct observation and actual use:

Individual Action

While teams or workgroups may be involved in creating any work product, a single person, an individual contributor in HR-speak, is ultimately responsible for delivery. It is the sum of those individual efforts producing, exchanging, and using mission-critical data that determines whether the execution of an initiative exceeds, meets, or fails to meet expectations.

This fact has important ramifications in CRISP™. Only the data that Consumers need from outside their Workstream or Entity is identified and managed. Those intersections, between function and entity, are called Nexus Points (NPs), and they are stored in the Nexus Point Exchange (NPX) Key Artifact.

Known Data Sets

At the highest level, the terms and conditions in the LOI (Letter of Intent), P&S (Purchase and Sale agreement), and, often, a Transition Service Agreement (TSA) drive CRISP™'s detail-level configurations. For example, provisions in the TSA might state that invoices for services rendered be delivered no later than 20 days after the end of the month when the service was rendered. This timing drives invoice preparation and its precursor, change management. This is mission-critical information contained in the deal docs, and knowable far in advance of any action needing to be taken.

For most individuals, the mission-critical data and information they need to do their part is limited and known well in advance of it actually being needed.

At a more granular level, determining precisely what is mission-critical data is relatively simple but often downplayed or ignored: If someone can't do their job in support of the initiative because they don't have the data they need, that's mission-critical. Reinforcing this notion is the fact that after decades of direct and indirect feedback from initiative performers, the number one reason given for delivery issues is SMEs not getting what they need in a timely manner from people outside (cross-functional/cross-entity, or CF/CE) their Workstreams.

Most folks working in this space will recognize complaints from technology units that the "business" doesn't get them what they need when they need it. But the fact is, the same scenario plays out between Operations and HR, Finance and Risk, and all other Workstream and Party combinations.

The design of CRISP™ addresses this problem head-on by focusing on only the CF/CE NPs; all other data exchanges happen within each workstream's organization, subject to their policies and processes. This limits any inter-workstream noise from bleeding into the larger initiative.

Not only that, there is a high probability that most, and in some cases all, of the mission-critical data already exists. It may be in various forms and locations, but it exists. CRISP™ protocols surface that data so that it can be shared and observed.

Known Process Sets

While much is said about how each M&A initiative is different, the fact is this: Process sets (what to do to achieve a result, like onboard an employee) at the macro level are well known, as are processes at the mid and micro levels, by at least one SME in any Party. If this were not true, every transaction would need to be approached as a new development exercise with unknowns far exceeding the knowns.

Here's an example of one obvious thing that is crucial to the success of most initiatives - getting people paid. And we'll use an acquisition transaction as the context to follow this explanation.

Hopefully, the individual steps and associated data are well known. HR has its role, as does IT, Finance, etc., first to determine who is getting paid, then how much and in what way... You get the picture. Everything related to processing payroll is already known and is practiced over and over again by the SMEs handling payroll. The only things missing are the names of those making the transition and their particulars.

Whether the Workstream is Finance (Treasury group setting up bank accounts for joint ventures or special projects) or IT (establishing email and network accounts), the processes and their corresponding CF/CE data requirements should be well known.

And where processes are codified through specialized forms or checklists, that data can be used by CRISP™ to identify deliverables produced as an outcome of the process. Where no forms exist, standards should be agreed upon quickly to ensure quality and efficiency.

Self-Inflicted Noise

Noise is present in all initiatives in a variety of ways, mostly from things like convoluted and incessant emails, irrelevant meetings, or recurring interruptions (voice, direct/instant messaging, email) by people looking for information or delivery status. It is almost always a result of historical behavior embedded in the way processes and policies are defined and followed (or not).

Put another way, most delays are caused unintentionally by noise generated by existing practices. In practical terms, workstream-related noise is often tamped down or worked around by the SMEs who encounter it every day. They know what's important and what to ignore. If they don't, performance issues are inevitable. But the noise with the greatest impact on any M&A transaction is the noise around CF/CE communication.

It's also worth noting that in CRISP™, there is no special treatment by role, rank, function, or priority when it comes to who needs things to do their job and who will be supplying them with what they need and when. So, a Producer from the Executive Workstream is no less responsible for delivering their Nexus Point Content (NPC) than anyone else in any other Workstream. This greatly reduces the noise most initiatives experience caused by well-intentioned attempts to prioritize deliverables using mechanisms and criteria outside of literal Producer-Consumer agreements.

Most importantly, there are few opportunities to ignore or work around noise when it comes from outside your Workstream or Entity. In this context, remember that noise in the form of potentially cascading interruptions is caused in significant ways by the search for missing information.

Embedded Dependencies

CRISP™ is organized around deliverables and, critically, the actual people responsible for those deliverables: those who procure or produce them (called Producers) and those who need them (called Consumers). How is this different than creating a story or defining a task, each of which may have a deliverable as its output? The real difference lies in determining just what deliverables are important.

Warning: The following is a radical departure from how the work for most initiatives is conceptualized and requires the suspension of disbelief that simplifying the approach can lead to greater accuracy.

Rather than investing time and money attempting to identify and load an exhaustive inventory of tasks and their dependencies into a project planning tool, ***CRISP™ uses the intrinsic knowledge that Producers and Consumers have of their own workloads to ensure no dependencies go unaddressed and that no gaps/disconnects exist.*** How does this happen?

CRISP™ uses prioritized Producer/Consumer vetting sessions to achieve initial alignment and surface any timing challenges relative to the initiative's events, reflected in the Milestone Chart Key Artifact. These sessions are followed by strategically defined alignment and readiness sessions, designed to surface any remaining gaps or conflicts that may exist.

Put simply, Consumers are responsible for voicing and registering their needs (NP properties) with the Producer of the deliverable (the Content or NPC), who assesses their workload to make promised delivery dates. If there is a conflict, it is resolved immediately through collaborative negotiations or escalated for a mandated resolution or special handling.

These orchestrated Producer-Consumer interactions, combined with two fast-following, all-hands alignment sessions and a final readiness session, are sufficient to ensure that all critical dependencies are accounted for, without resorting to separate documents or administratively-heavy planning/scheduling tools.

Non-Encroaching Processes

One last thing for clarity: Individual Workstreams are expected to use whatever methods they find effective to organize and sequence **their** work according to the process and policy of their overarching Workstream, **provided** they do not force other functional areas to conform to their way of doing things. Here's an example:

IT units are notorious for gathering users together so that they (the IT folks, Consumers in this case) can complete **their** requirements or configuration documents on **their** schedule. Because there is a high probability that not all the information will be available in a single session, discontinuities and the necessity for follow-ups are introduced into the workflow on both the Producer and Consumer sides of the data. And because there is normally some overlap or duplication of data with varying degrees of formal assignment of ownership, the process instantly becomes inefficient with a commensurate drop in quality (multiple sources of truth creating multiple opportunities for error).

CRISP™ solves this by acknowledging that if the cross-functional information IT is after is known in advance (and if it isn't, *that* might be an issue), Consumers and Producers should be able to establish delivery dates and Content expectations without necessitating time-expensive general requirement meetings. IT then gets its info when it needs it as a Consumer through the NPX, just like everyone else.

Operating Assumptions

Successfully adopting CRISP™ depends on understanding and accepting several key assumptions related to the environments in which it will be used. These assumptions should be validated during initial buy-in before moving forward.

Subject Matter Experts (SMEs)

It's worth repeating that, beyond the strategic and tactical decisions made to address the financial, legal, and operational aspects of a transaction before it occurs, achieving lasting success relies entirely on the coordinated efforts of individual contributors: the subject matter experts (SMEs). Because of this, it is imperative that SMEs understand their respective roles and responsibilities needed for service of the transaction type. This seems like common sense and is often assumed to be the case, without any testing or validation of the current reality. In the context of CRISP™, this is a critical assumption.

CRISP™ counts on the fact that SMEs inherently understand the complexity (or simplicity) of the things they need that impact the timing and quality of **their** deliverables. For example, a Finance SME who is responsible for establishing new bank accounts needs data like the legal company name, a banking contact, and tax ID number. Fortunately, for most Colleagues, this understanding reduces to a handful of data or information they need from individuals **outside** their Workstream.

The collective CF/CE SME understanding is accounted for and embedded in CRISP™ data and vetted through intentional collaboration processes. By focusing on and tracking each individual's cross-functional requirements, **the need to create and then maintain arbitrary cross-functional schedules, plans, or dependencies is eliminated**.

This is not to say that CRISP™ replaces all planning or scheduling exercises, far from it.

Workstream/SME-specific schedules and plans are unique and very much are expected to be developed/managed **in those Workstreams**. Failures stemming from poor Workstream planning become readily apparent as issues with Producer NPC delivery are immediately visible. But at the enterprise or program level, the effort and cost of performing this type of detailed planning, data collection, and continuous updating are unnecessary with CRISP™.

Put another way, there is no need to overlay a control system (with its ongoing maintenance) when each individual Producer and Consumer understands the impact of dates and deliverables on their ability to perform not just for the initiative, but also their daily jobs. This understanding is codified and maintained in the NPX at the level of granularity that Consumers need and with dates Producers can commit to.

Changes to Nexus Points (NPs) and their related Content delivery are an expected occurrence during the arc of any initiative. Responsibility for communicating these changes lies solely with the Producer.

Since CRISP™ lets Producers know precisely who will be consuming their Content, timing or content changes can be targeted to a few individuals (who will ratify or renegotiate if necessary and possible) vs aggregated change notices broadcast in a shotgun fashion, hoping that whoever needs to see the change picks it up.

Functional Workstreams and Their Leadership

Functional Workstream Leads are accountable for the deliverables their Colleagues are responsible for. Based on this assumption, the need to overlay a new/different accountability structure to accommodate the initiative, typical of traditional approaches, is unnecessary.

Traditional command-and-control projects typically have a separate governance structure, such as a PMO or similar organization, to try and manage cross-functional task-based dependencies. While there is no reason a Workstream can't adopt that form of management within its boundaries, CRISP™ does not need any additional governance mechanisms beyond the defined protocols and artifacts in order to meet expectations.

Here, the rules are straightforward: Producers are **responsible** for delivering NPC and communicating any changes to the Consumers of those NPs. Workstream Leads (WLs) are **accountable** for issues connected to the delivery of any NP.

For clarity, an IMO is neither responsible nor accountable for ensuring deliverables meet expectations; this falls squarely on Consumers, Producers, and, if necessary, Workstream Leads. Note: Actual IMO role and responsibility is described later.

Following this approach, IMO messaging around late or missing information is simplified, putting follow-up responsibility directly on the parties with compliance authority rather than an intermediary with limited influence.

It should not go unmentioned that this assumption also has important speed implications. Avoiding potential delays by eliminating escalation activity that adds unnecessary communication and reaction time to the initiative naturally reduces the time it takes to complete the Initiative.

Transaction-Specific Information/Data

The vast majority of the specific information/data needed to configure systems, execute procurement activities, on-board employees, etc., in service of any Transaction should be well known by the SMEs and their parent workstreams far in advance of the Transaction close. CRISP™ assumes that the majority of this CF/CE content can be articulated and recorded in a common tool (the NPX) through easy-to-perform Producer/Consumer collaboration sessions prior to actual execution occurring.

The speed and efficiency impact of this assumption is most noticeable by the re-casting of traditional independent requirement gathering siloes and documents into a unified, data-focused repository. For future transaction activity, the existing documentation reinforcing this assumption will only improve with continued usage and refinement.

Culture Celebrating Collaboration and Personal Responsibility

Not surprisingly, CRISP™ relies on people understanding what they are obligated to do and then doing it when they say they will. The model reinforces the aspirational and literal notion that it is in everyone's best interest to do what needs to be done as efficiently and effectively as possible. Everyone benefits.

This reinforcement comes from the synergistic design of artifacts and protocols that recognize and cater to individual Colleagues' requirements and responsibilities, focusing on eliciting and codifying what they need (Consumers) and matching those needs directly to the folks who will deliver them (Producers). Making these relationships explicit and visible naturally creates personal connections and obligations between Colleagues.

This is in contrast to top-down, command-and-control management models, where Producers are often hidden behind generic workstreams or task labels, and understanding who the actual Consumers are is never formally articulated, or their role is abstracted as an arbitrarily decided task dependency value.

However, this is not the only dynamic at play.

Every change initiative (what M&A transactions are ultimately about) surfaces behavior that is driven by cultural norms that may be inefficient or counterproductive, no matter how strong or valid a proposed strategy may be. From experience, companies particularly vulnerable to this behavior have both lengthy histories and policies that reward employee tenure over performance. Although "us vs them" and "that's not how we do things" behavior can also be present in younger companies where new hires or contractors comprise the bulk of the workers and turf protection is in high gear.

Here's one example of how this behavior manifests.

At the start of a carve-out initiative, the Buyer's contracted management consultant announced that they needed unrestricted access to all the Seller's SMEs across all functional areas or scheduling issues would surely occur. This type of unilateral demand matched with an undesirable outcome is not uncommon.

For the Seller, accepting this arrangement would mean a constant stream of random interruptions to folks doing their day jobs; not likely to be well received. The consultant was disabused of this idea by agreeing to use the Request List Key Artifact to formally make requests explaining what they were looking for and when they needed it, which were then triaged by the IMOs. More often than not the requests could be handled without disrupting the Seller's SMEs at all.

The Peter Drucker quote "culture eats strategy for breakfast" is also instructive in this context, highlighting its negative effects: ingrained organizational biases that can retard or block changes necessary to realize significant improvements. Fixing those biases is out of scope for this book.

Minimal Administrative Overhead and Resources

In most cases, the SMEs delivering service to the initiative are doing so in addition to their regular jobs. So the administrative overhead and resources required to monitor transactions and exchange data that are imposed on each Colleague must be minimal.

One way this can happen is by allowing the Workstream SMEs to plan and manage their own work without intervention by the IMO. Adopting this approach removes both the administrative need to understand why data is due or late, and the administrative burden placed on Consumers and Producers to report interim status (outside of the practices/policies of their department or workstream).

Focusing on just the information that needs to be exchanged **between** workstreams and entities eliminates the need and expense of managing or adopting a common method to monitor disparate work processes under a monolithic program/project planning structure, which can add unnecessary expense and effort.

Embracing Efficient Communication

Each NPX record containing content has a unique identifier that will travel with it throughout the initiative and, perhaps, other future initiatives.

Since each piece of shared data is identified with an unambiguous label, communication can become more efficient and precise, reducing repeated miscommunication, explanations, and requests. This, of course, assumes the Producers and Consumers embrace a new way of communicating as part of the initiative's mandate. Think "doing it by the numbers." Here's an example illustrating this point.

30 days after integration has begun, Sally, a Buyer Finance SME, needs a piece of data from the Seller's Legal department. The traditional way of getting this information, assuming Sally knows who in Legal to contact, is for her to send an email and/or an IM/DM describing what she is looking for. Then she waits for the Legal resource to respond, hopefully with the correct information.

If Sally does not know who provides the data, the timeline is extended to include the additional effort needed to locate the data source. This can get way more complicated, convoluted, and costly, depending on what data is being sought and from where, and of course, Sally's description of what she's after.

In contrast, here's how that same request is handled using CRISP™: Sally 1st checks the NPX, and finds a description of the Content she needs. She immediately sees when and how that Content will be available and who is delivering it, assuming it has not already been provided. Last, Sally tags the item to formally record her need as a Consumer (explicitly putting the Producer on notice) and notes its identifying NPX ID in case she needs to refer to it later.

There is no need for Sally to spend time crafting an individual request for the information; it is already established that this data is needed by others, and as part of the process, the description, format, and delivery date have already been vetted. Sally now only needs to check the NPX for the item's delivery to get the data. She can also see the Consumer tags of any other people who need the data, eliminating redundant or duplicated messaging for both requests and responses.

Finding Mission Critical Data With and Without CRISP™

Without CRISP™

	Activity / Wait time	Elapsed time
Sally Sends Email / DM	1:30	1:30
Wait for Response	? minutes to days	1:30 + 1 day
Receive and evaluate response	30 secs to determine faulty response	2:00 + 1 day
Resend Email / DM or call for clarity	1:00	3:00 + 1 day
Wait for Response	? minutes to days	3:00 + 1 day + ½ day

Total elapsed time: 1.5 days + 3 minutes

With CRISP™

	Activity / Wait time	Elapsed time
Sally Checks NPX	0:30	0:30
Needed Data Found & Reviewed	0:30	1:00
Use Data or wait for Delivery	0:00	1:00

Total elapsed time: 1 minute

Efficient communication relies on predictability and repeatability, or "practice." For organizations with dedicated M&A staff who are continuously active, practice happens throughout the year. But CRISP™ also supports transactions that are naturally intermittent over extended time periods.

When the opportunities for practice are separated by considerable lengths of time, adopting the common reference strategy tied directly to the required data that CRISP™ provides bridges the gap. Otherwise, the same pattern of random asks and interruptions is what predictably repeats.

A common reference model also enables multiple transactions to be represented simultaneously, allowing potential scaling should more than one transaction present itself during the same time period.

Finally, over time, tracking deliverables this way also provides a rich data set for analysis, resulting in even greater understanding and opportunities for targeted refinement activities.

Base

- Individual action
- Known data and process sets
- Self-inflicted noise
- Embedded dependencies
- Non-encroaching processes

Operating Summary

To quickly summarize the key assumptions behind CRISP™:

- SME competency
- Workstream lead accountability
- Data predictability
- Collaborative trust

- Minimal administrative overhead
- Embracing model efficiency

Each of these assumptions plays a key role in the adoption of CRISP™ and, in turn, in a Transaction occurring with as little messaging friction and effort as possible.

CRISP™ vs Traditional Approaches

CRISP™ does not follow the well-worn techniques most enterprise projects and programs use. Communication among individuals lies at its core. Not just any communication, but specifically individual exchanges between functions and among parties. By focusing on mission critical communication at the individual level, many typical documents and activities called for by playbooks become unnecessary.

Here's a comparison of some common activities and their CRISP™ equivalents:

Typical M&A Activities	Typical Frequency	CRISP™ Equivalent
Status-focused joint meetings - work-stream	Weekly	Not needed
Status-focused joint meetings – steering	Bi-Weekly	Not needed
SME/Work-stream-driven group requirement gathering meetings	Multiple	Individual consumer/ producer-driven alignment meetings (attendance optional)
Mandatory large group planning sessions	Multiple	2 all-hands readiness sessions (attending 1 is required)

Typical M&A Activities	Typical Frequency	CRISP™ Equivalent
Task dependency monitoring and plan maintenance	Daily	Not needed
Status reporting - work-stream	Weekly by work-stream	Not needed
Status reporting preparation	Weekly by colleague	Not needed
Initiative-level time keeping	Weekly by colleague	Not needed
Data/information requests by phone calls, emails, direct messaging	Ad hoc; multiple	Not needed
"When will this be delivered" phone calls, emails, direct messaging	Ad hoc; multiple	Not needed
External vendor information inquiries	Ad hoc; multiple	Reduced or eliminated external vendor information inquiries

So how can this be? By truly focusing on individuals and communication, much of the traditional, factory-based, management model becomes unnecessary. Why?

Traditional planning and management methods and their artifacts, including Waterfall/Predictive and Agile/Iterative (in all its flavors), are not inherently focused on communication between parties. They are fundamentally organized around tasks, identifying and documenting dependencies, and attempting to estimate and monitor pre-delivery work in order to predict when delivery will (or will not) occur. As a result, these methods have a number of unavoidable outcomes:

1. They increase the administrative burden on employees by forcing compliance with low-value reporting tasks and processes, which introduce messaging time lags, inaccurate time reporting, and general noise in the process (even Agile methods suffer from this).
2. They shift focus to task performance and away from the production of a deliverable for a Consumer.
3. They create a false sense of control that what exists in the plan (from the initial estimate to the current 'status') will become or is reality.
4. They are difficult to scale and very difficult to adequately communicate changes to affected participants.

In some cases, these outcomes are exacerbated by reliance on ad hoc platforms like Slack or Teams, where information exchange happens with little structure or standardization—the two things required to increase speed while ensuring quality.

Agile

Agile methods are first and foremost iterative. They make progress by iterating through a series of ceremonies and artifacts to reach deliverables that are newly defined.

While this is an effective model for software or product development where new things are being created, iteration to reach a deliverable, no matter how short the interval, does not work well for most M&A initiatives, especially across Workstreams and Entities. This is because the Initiative is contract-driven, with legally binding deadlines, rather than aspiration-driven, as in software development. But more importantly, Agile's fundamental benefit—dealing incrementally with unknowns as they occur—is the opposite of what is needed for the efficient execution of most M&A transactions with known data.

Waterfall/Predictive

Attempting to manage by GANTT chart (or similar dependency-based prediction methods) in the context of executing M&A transactions, while arguably a slightly better fit due to the finite number of identifiable elements, it is also ineffective and costly. Here's why:

The usefulness of any predictive method heavily depends on:

1) accuracy of the underlying duration or work estimates.
2) accuracy and timeliness of the defined dependencies.
3) timely and accurate collection of interim status data.

Deficiencies in any of these items will yield information that can be wildly inaccurate or misleading, and regardless of the purpose, should not be used for planning or decision-making unless the deficiencies can be truly mitigated.

Plus, when tasks are late and dependencies change, the underlying map/plan must be updated, recalculated, and republished. In the context of a one-time event that a Transaction represents, a purely predictive approach ends up being an expensive investment to get what most often is an illusion of precision or control of tasks, rather than the reality of getting deliverables into the hands of those who need them.

> Timecards in and of themselves can be a source of noise, which increases steadily starting right after the task/project being worked on is complete. The more time that passes between when the work is performed and the point at which it is recorded, the greater the potential error in reporting. According to neuroscience, after 1 hour, more than 50% of what was done is forgotten. In 24 hours, recall drops by about 67% without additional reinforcement. After a week, the typical time recording cadence of many organizations, only the tasks performed near the entry date will be a reasonably correct reflection of what happened.

Using this potentially flawed time-against-task data, a status calculation of % complete is made, even though for business planners, the estimate on which that duration is based is most likely an arbitrary, "Get this done by…"

Underlying Neuroscience

In addition to communication theory, recent findings in neuroscience, particularly where decision-making and concentration are concerned, are also embedded in CRISP™. Chief among these are those elements related to stress, reward mechanisms, and attention. What follows is a radically simplified and compressed explanation of how CRISP™ is designed to positively affect several neurological functions.

Your Brain Health Depends on Your Colleagues

The brain wants to conserve energy. It takes mental energy (consumption of brain fuel) to do work. If fuel runs low, quality suffers. If fuel runs out, work stops.

When people are concentrating on their work, their brains consume and direct energy efficiently. But humans love novelty. So, when we are interrupted by something new, we reward ourselves with a hit of happiness (dopamine), while energy is consumed to divert focus and ascertain what, if any, action needs to be taken in response to the new stimulus.

Once the diversion is disposed of (or not), a switch back to the original focus is made, which not only consumes energy itself, but leads to even more energy being used to figure out where you left off. The longer you are away, the more expensive (fuel and time-wise) it is to return, and the more often you switch, the lower your fuel supply becomes. This is what "multi-tasking" looks like from a neuroscience point of view.

CRISP™ directly addresses multi-tasking triggers (interruptions/noise) by solving the number one issue that causes those interruptions in the first place: asking for and delivering information. In the context of Transactions, NPs and their usage protocols form a potent mechanism to tamp down noise by providing a faster, higher-quality substitute for "Where do I find _____?"

In addition to interruptions, due to the nature of almost any Transaction, work is going to be added on top of people's existing jobs. If existing workloads are already causing stress, accommodating more work will be challenging and should be factored into transition expectations. CRISP™ helps solve this issue by allowing Producers to set their own delivery dates, within the guardrails of the milestones and the needs of the Consumers.

See Appendix B for more neuroscience details.

Cultural Requirements

As mentioned previously, CRISP™ operates best when the underlying cultural environment is based on and supports two fundamental behaviors:

1. Trust
2. Accountability

Trust between Colleagues, Workstreams, and Entities is essential, and is grounded in the expectation that Consumers will voice their needs and Producers will honor their commitments. It is as simple as that.

Accountability is necessary because ambiguity in describing deliverables causes unnecessary confusion, delays, and interruptions. Clear accountability speeds up the process by eliminating any doubt as to who is responsible, with clear lines and conditions for escalation/elevation defined should issues arise. CRISP™ will fail fastest in organizations where who is accountable is up for debate.

Note: It is not uncommon for Workstream Leads to feel that IMO/PMO organizations should be responsible for chasing their SMEs who are late or otherwise deficient in delivering their NPCs. This is contrary to the CRISP™ efficiency design and rule of accountability. Since time is of the essence with any transaction, any indirect routing of NPC issues necessarily delays correcting the problem.

CRISP™'s escalation protocol is based on the notion that if a Producer is late with their NPC, the WL is the one accountable for chasing its delivery. WLs have the organizational clout within their Workstream to take measures that the Producer will be compelled to respond to. Interposing another person or persons in the process with little organizational influence wastes precious time, full stop.

Shared History: Importance and Influence

M&A transactions involving organizational transformations are greatly influenced by the shared history of the Colleagues within the Entities. Shared history affects Initiative execution in the following ways:

Communication Shorthand

- Employees within Workstreams have their own vocabularies and shorthand for referring to things and people in and outside their domain. Over time, the repetitive nature of communication and sharing of experiences creates abbreviated versions and names for things that affect the employee's ability to do their job. This shorthand is also developed with cross-functional employees in much the same way.
- The longer the tenure, the deeper in meaning and more abbreviated the shorthand becomes.
- In this context, the NPX serves as a special-purpose CF/CE taxonomy, bridging understanding between functions and entities and allowing a place for synonyms or nicknames to be part of the content.

Separation Dynamics

- Depending on the organization, separation dynamics take on several different forms, impacted by the nature of the transaction. Here are three common examples:

- Where a wholly-owned subsidiary of an entire division is being spun off or divested.
- Where an existing group needs to merge with another existing group.
- Where material decreases in headcount are anticipated.
- CRISP™'s contribution to each form is the same, and that is to make the separation as pain-free as possible by lowering the possibility that something will be missed.

Post-Close Support and Contact

- Divestitures or acquisitions often require the Seller to provide transition services. Efficiently providing these services requires careful upfront planning as:
    - Continued burdening of Seller's resources must be factored into the allocation strategy.
    - Knowledge transfer must be performed and documented against the contractual obligations.
    - The "final" transition may occur months or even years after all knowledge is transferred and no further service is required.
- This is especially true when completion of the deal relies on the performance of regulatory bodies (permits, licensing, etc.), which may not be fully realized before the formal deal close, but remain as open issues until resolved.
- CRISP™'s Protocols help streamline post-close activities by providing explicit instructions related to managing TSA's and KT.

Mitigating the Risk of Using Yesterday's Playbook in Today's World

Traditional initiative playbooks were created for slower, simpler, less interconnected operating environments. Many rely on heavy status reporting, generalized work plans, or meeting-driven alignment that cannot keep pace with today's information volume or cross-entity complexity. When those legacy approaches are applied to modern initiatives, they create predictable failure modes.

Risk Categories Relevant to Initiatives

What follows is a condensed list of initiative risk categories and their underlying causes.

Risk Category	Description
Execution	Breakdowns in cross-functional or cross-entity delivery due to unclear ownership, misaligned timing, delayed access, inconsistent messaging, or rework.
Strategic	Flawed or incomplete assumptions underlying the initiative's direction, objectives, or expected outcomes.
Operational	Gaps in systems, processes, or workflows that prevent the initiative from functioning as required.
Informational	Delays, inaccuracies, omissions, or inconsistent interpretations of essential information.
Compliance and Governance	Failure to meet contractual, regulatory, or TSA-related obligations or to maintain required controls.
Cultural and People	Confusion, misalignment, or disengagement among contributors due to unclear expectations or communication.

How CRISP™ Mitigates Risk

Using the categories defined above, here's how CRISP™ addresses each one:

Execution Risk Mitigation

CRISP™'s sole focus is on providing an optimized structure based on the following:

- Clear ownership at the individual level
- Alignment of ownership, purpose, and timing through the NPX
- Actual dependencies expressed through negotiated due dates
- Standardized messaging behavior that reduces interpretation variance
- Fewer alignment meetings because deliverables are clean, consistent, and predictable
- Prioritization and visibility for Consumer needs and Producer loading through calculated Impact Scores

Strategy Risk Mitigation

CRISP™ can't do anything to prevent the eventual outcome of a bad deal thesis or incomplete or faulty due diligence. Depending on when in the initiative arc CRISP™ is put into action, in some cases it can provide early warning that something is wrong, particularly where compliance issues based on cultural conflicts occur.

Operational Risk Mitigation

- Milestone Schedule establishes clear synchronization points
- Application Matrix clarifies environments, interfaces, testing and training needs
- TSA Agreement Matrix defines and tracks Buyer and Seller post-close obligations

- Colleague Roster ensures proper communication paths and access controls

Information Risk Mitigation

- Consolidated CF/CE Requests prevent information drift
- NPX centralizes information exchange at the Producer and Consumer level
- Deliverables become consistent, current, and single-sourced
- Parallel trackers and version conflicts are eliminated

Compliance and Governance Risk Mitigation

- Ground-level monitoring of TSA obligations and change handling artifacts
- Standardized protocols for access and communication
- Field guides defining and reinforcing consistent behavior
- Artifacts that operate inside existing systems to support governance

Cultural and People Risk Mitigation

- Clear, initiative-wide messaging behavior
- Early alignment on expectations and timing
- Defined channels for questions and approvals
- Reduced frustration through predictable information flow

Risk Summary

Effective governance depends on clarity, predictability, and consistent communication. Initiative performance degrades when ownership, purpose, or timing is uncertain, and when information moves through informal or inconsistent channels.

The risks outlined above show how outdated or task-based playbooks contribute to misalignment, rework, and unnecessary friction. CRISP™ addresses these issues through structured communication practices, clear and direct routing of decisions, and artifacts designed to eliminate interpretation variance across contributors and entities.

This creates the conditions required for strong governance. When assignments are explicit, when information is aligned before work begins, and when contributors use the same communication patterns, governance shifts from reactive oversight to proactive assurance. The Governance chapter explains how these behaviors support initiative-wide stability, reinforce compliance requirements, and create a reliable operating structure for all contributors involved in execution.

NOTES

Governance

CRISP™ reinforces the common-sense notion that stable governance is a necessary requirement for efficient and effective execution of an Initiative.

Note that "stable" does not necessarily equate with "rigid". Stable in this context means well-understood and consistently applied protocols (rules of interaction) that are agreed to and carried out by people in specific roles.

Organizational Structures

The purpose of a CRISP™ organization structure is two-fold:

1. To provide unambiguous escalation paths and mechanisms.
2. To define major Workstreams and identify their leads.

The organization has two parallel layers: the Workstream Layer and the SteerCo Layer. For consistency, this basic organization should be mirrored between Buyer and Seller, such that all Workstream Leads have direct counterparts. Note: This may not happen cleanly (1-1) due to organizational size and maturity; the model accommodates these occurrences by explicitly exposing where there are mismatches and solving for them by codifying exactly who the matching Colleagues are.

https://crispmethod.com/crisp-organization-structure/?cm_id=omae

Workstreams

Workstreams are meant to be aligned in a best effort manner following existing organizational patterns (reporting structures), acknowledging special cases where appropriate. Workstreams, thus defined, are homes to the individual Subject Matter Expert Colleagues on whom success depends. The reason for this structure is to leverage organizational norms when escalation is required.

For example, the illustrated workstream design includes Payroll under either Finance or HR workstreams, rather than separating Payroll as a workstream of its own. Another organization may do the opposite. Regardless, accountability for Producer deliverables falls to the related Workstream Lead.

Steering Committees

The Steering Committee (SteerCo) in CRISP™ is deliberately narrow in scope and designed to maximize impact while minimizing time.

In many traditionally managed initiatives, steering committees evolve into catch-all forums for interim status updates, presentations, and broad discussion. This dilutes their effectiveness and consumes significant executive time without materially advancing execution.

However, by shifting the bulk of reporting to the NPX and restricting the SteerCo remit to escalations and executive interactions, CRISP™ reduces the number and length of meetings while sharpening focus. This results in a structure that preserves leadership attention for the highest-value decisions, rather than reviewing information already available to every Colleague.

Steering committees have three primary functions under CRISP™:

1. Negotiating
2. Handling escalated issues that could not be solved at lower levels
3. Realigning people, Workstreams, or the Initiative as a whole

SteerCo negotiations are necessary when unresolved differences between Workstreams or Entities (and possibly their SMEs) occur. For any initiative, these differences can be triggered by an infinite array of things. Here are a couple of common examples:

- The Buyer's finance workstream realizes that the original estimate of support needed for payroll operations is not enough to cover what needs to be done.
- The Seller's IT workstream is being overloaded with ad hoc and sometimes duplicate requests from the Buyer's IT consultants that are outside of the agreed-upon scope of service or IP access.
- The Buyer's efforts to staff a new Sales organization are not progressing fast enough to meet the agreed-upon transition timeline.

Acting as an escalation endpoint, a SteerCo provides the final decision authority when Colleague or Workstream issues can not be fully addressed during normal interactions.

For organizations using CRISP™, the SteerCo's time spent dealing with escalations should be minimal. Here are some typical escalations whose importance typically rises to the level of a SteerCo:

- Differences in approach between IT organizations and external consultants.
- Repeated delivery failures due to lack of available talent.
- Conflicting TSA interpretations.

Lastly, during any M&A initiative, there may be a need to reset expectations or realign Colleagues. SteerCos are the source of this action. These resets or realignments can be isolated to a single Workstream or extend and affect the entire deal. Here are some familiar causes.

- During due diligence, the Buyer or Seller Legal and Finance teams need more time to review submitted material, altering previously agreed-upon target dates.
- Pre-close, delays caused by regulatory bodies.
- Post-close, key personnel attrition creating performance or delivery gaps.

CRISP™ attempts to minimize low-value executive involvement wherever it can. The Protocols around how one of the most expensive meeting types operates focus on keeping the initiative moving, not looking backward.

PEOPLE AND ROLES

Keeping with the goal of reducing the noise between Colleagues and accelerating the speed at which information is available, using the CRISP™ model does not typically require the use of anything more than a dedicated Initiative Administrator (IA) role. The title of Administrator, rather than Manager, is deliberate.

Initiative Administrator

By design, an initiative using CRISP™ does **not** call for the deep talent or broad skills of a heroic project or program manager. Nor does it (or should it) require in-depth subject matter expertise in any particular area. The foundational rules of CRISP™ are simple, and the process architecture is, for the most part, self-defining and self-maintaining. This leaves the IA with the following responsibilities:

1) Scheduling and conducting CRISP™ events
2) Generating reminders to Producers of NPC due-dates*
3) Scheduling and facilitating alignment, readiness, SteerCo, and Workstream lead meetings
4) Preparing and delivering TSA invoices**
5) Publishing Initiative communication messages*
6) Gatekeeping and grooming the NPX for relevance, Producership, and Consumer accuracy
7) Observing and arbitrating select CF/CE meetings to spot gaps in NP representation and monitor and enforce TSA compliance
8) Coordinating and negotiating TSA change requests, including item terminations**
9) Coaching Colleagues and Stakeholders on CRISP™ protocols

* May be automated. ** May be partially automated.

It's recommended that, at least to start, the IA be a single resource dedicated to a single Initiative. In those instances where initiatives are plentiful, after a single deal using CRISP™, each subsequent use gets faster and easier, allowing IAs to potentially administer more than one initiative at a time.

Note: A single IA should be able to easily handle a Colleague Roster up to 150, with about 50 of those acting as Producers. This estimate assumes all the elements of CRISP™ are in place. If the NPX reporting is automated, the numbers can be higher. Keep this next part in mind when thinking about who is assigned the IA role.

Choke Point: The IA role has a single known choke point—the aspirational goal of direct participation in all Producer-Consumer sessions. For particularly large initiatives or those where there are lots of different Producers, IAs can be overloaded with too many Producer-Consumer meetings to facilitate by themselves.

There are three options to solve this problem:

1. Low NP count Producer sessions can be combined to reduce the overall session count, though this may not be enough to solve the issue.
2. Low NP count Producers forego their sessions (creating potential alignment issues, but still workable), also to lower the overall session count.
3. Providing CRISP™-trained business analysts or similarly trained idle project managers to shepherd this once-per-initiative process. This is the recommended best practice.

One final point. Like any Colleague serving as an administrative focal point, the IAs need the full-throated backing of the highest executives connected with the Initiative.

Minimally, these are the individuals who make up the SteerCos or, in some cases, function organizationally above the SteerCo. When IAs are needed to act as dispute arbiters or compliance enforcers, that upper-level support is essential to lend credibility to the role. Without it, Colleagues will quickly turn to paths of least resistance, which can quickly undermine the efficiency and quality attributes of CRISP™.

Workstream Leaders

Workstream Leaders play a pivotal role in CRISP™, as they are ultimately accountable for ensuring their NPC Producers deliver as expected. But they are also a group that acts as:

- negotiators between other Workstream Leads.
- initial escalation points for late or problematic NPC delivery.
- in-flight, up and downstream alignment facilitators.
- promoters (and if needed, enforcers) of CRISP™ protocols.

Negotiator

All Initiatives have all manner of negotiated items that affect their smooth execution, both within the same party and across the transaction. The WL group handles those items that affect progress at the Workstream level. If the WLs are unable to reach an agreement, the issue is elevated to the SteerCo's next session for disposition, unless the item is time-sensitive and warrants a special session be called.

Escalation Point

Since the WLs are accountable for their Workstream's deliverables, it's important that they have not only the organizational backing to compel Producers to perform, but also the coaching skills to effectively remind Consumers on their teams of CRISP™ protocols. Of particular importance is coaching specifically around surfacing NPs to avoid data hoarding.

Facilitator

During the course of the Initiative, WLs may need to facilitate or participate in facilitation sessions between their workstream Colleagues and others. A few examples of this are:

1) HR clarification sessions between Parties where coverage mismatches exist
2) Knowledge transfer between Parties
3) Validation of plans and strategies related to transition strategies

Promoter

In addition to handling Colleague escalation activities, WLs are critical communication sources used to keep contributors engaged throughout the initiative.

One of the ways this is done is by repeatedly asking a simple question: "What specific data or information do you need to do your job relative to the Initiative, and if the source of that data is coming from outside your Workstream, is it represented in the NPX?" Ideally, the question should be asked at every opportunity CF/CE Workstream Colleagues meet and incorporated into every meeting's closing "Next Steps" discussion.

Another way WLs act as promoters is by diligently referring Colleagues to the NPX or other key documents when information questions arise. "Have you checked the NPX?" should be the 1st response to this type of inquiry. This way, instead of providing the information directly (potentially creating an alternate source of truth), the WL guides the Colleague to the actual source of truth, and possibly a missing piece of information.

Steering Committee Members

Steering Committee members under CRISP™ play an important role in the orderly execution of Initiatives. Here are the major contributions they are responsible for:

1) Negotiations between Parties establishing deal requirements reflected in the final P&S and TSA agreements
2) Initiative Decision segment of the Preparation Phase, leading to the P&S execution—the 'Go' signal.
3) Post-close Execution Phases
    a. Workstream escalation points
    b. Negotiation of disputes between and among Parties
3) Final Close-out
    a. Approval endpoint

Using CRISP™, the recommended cadence for SteerCo sessions is a standing meeting scheduled every two weeks. This cadence can be reduced to monthly when CRISP™ is fully adopted and Colleagues are executing against well-defined objectives.

If SteerCo activity (joint or separate) is anticipated to be needed more frequently, discovery and discussion as to why should be done as quickly as possible, as it can signal potential optimization/blocking/trust issues whose risks could be addressed earlier or elsewhere.

The most common reason for greater than bi-weekly meetings is that the SteerCo feels it needs to insert itself directly into the execution flow, which, unless justified because of resource constraints or continuing escalation needs, will naturally retard progress and could be unnecessary.

See the section on Organizational structures for additional details.

Employee Data Handler

For any initiative where people will be affected, CRISP™ recommends the appointment or hiring of an Employee Data Handler to serve as an interface to all Consumers where employee information needs to be exchanged. Their responsibilities include:

1) Controlling access to the Employee Matrix document
2) Recording and disposition of requests for protected employee PII (Personally Identifiable Information) data not available in the Employee Matrix that will occur in the normal course of events. This serves as a security check and audit control point.

Existing functions suited for the EDH role include payroll, HR or support clerks, or analysts. When the Employee Matrix and related Protocol are in use, this role has been shown to consume less than an hour a week.

The administrative burden connected with requests for employee information drops considerably when non-confidential information is readily available to those Colleagues who need it.

[Optional] Executive Steering Committee Members

All transactions require the involvement of senior executives. Acting as signatories or decision gates, they play an active role. It is important to note that CRISP™ draws no distinction between, for instance, an HR Analyst delivering a cost-benefit analysis for Finance and a Senior VP giving the green light to proceed on some aspect of the initiative. Each has NPC to deliver that is critical to initiative execution.

For this reason, there is no CRISP™ requirement for an Executive Steering Committee, or its equivalent. The need for a separate class of steering committee (and the attendant scheduling and facilitation) is only necessary if truly compelling reasons exist. Otherwise, establishing another level of escalation above the SteerCo can retard progress and add unnecessary facilitation and reporting work to the initiative.

Issue Resolution and Elevation/Escalation

CRISP™'s primary purpose is to make the execution process as seamless as possible, but there are always issues that do not resolve on their own and need additional voices for a solution to be reached. Here's an example taken from an actual initiative of how common issues end up in front of senior executives.

It's clearly a *non-happy path* scenario:

Barry was a Producer who agreed with his Consumers to deliver his piece on Day 0. There were 3 Consumers for Barry's work product. This is explicitly reflected by an NP in the NPX.

Day 0+1 arrived, and the NP record in the NPX was not updated with Content and its delivery date. Barry's WL contacted him to determine the issue and resolve the delay ASAP. They also checked with the Consumers to ascertain the delay impact. This was escalation #1.

Consumers said the delay impact was high. Resolution was not timely. The WL then escalated the issue to Barry's boss. This was escalation #2. Turns out, Barry was getting conflicting priorities from his boss, who put Barry's other work ahead of the initiative. Barry's boss was insistent that Barry's schedule could not be altered.

Barry's WL then contacted the Initiative Administrator to alert them to the issue impasse. The IA already knew something was up when Barry's NP slipped, but it is up to the WL to attempt the 1st resolution. The IMO set the threshold for intervention, in this case 3 days without movement. The IA decided whether the issue needed to go to the SteerCo, which one, and how. Given Barry's boss's position, the decision was to escalate to the internal SteerCo. This was escalation #3. Since waiting for the next SteerCo meeting would take too long given the immediacy of the issue, an emergency session was convened.

During the emergency session, it was discovered that a side-deal between the Buyer and Seller CFOs had created another NP deliverable for Barry that was not recorded in the NPX, making it invisible. The internal CFO had made the side-deal a priority and communicated that choice to Barry's boss, hence the entrenched position.

Given the severity of the delay and the breach of protocol, the decision was made to bring this situation up at the next joint SteerCo, where both CFOs would be available to negotiate a solution and reaffirm their support of the engagement rules. This was escalation #4. In the meantime, now understanding the criticality of the situation (and perhaps to head off future criticism), the CFO added help for Barry to get both deliverables back on track.

Obviously, there are endless variations of how this scenario could have played out, but the main point is this: Time does not help a late deliverable, and the sooner action is taken to achieve resolution, the better. Each escalation point attempts to get satisfaction before moving on to the next level, and they are handled as rapidly and automatically as possible.

Special Note: Why Workstream Leads Should Never be Producers.

Here's the issue: Producers are responsible for delivering NPC at the agreed-upon dates and in the agreed-upon format. If a Producer fails to deliver by the date they commit to or there are quality issues with the NPC, CRISP™ calls for the **immediate** escalation of the missed commitments to the Workstream Lead for disposition.

If the WL and Producer are the same person, this creates a situation where the next level of elevation (the SteerCo) needs to be engaged. This always introduces time lags into the process, as the SteerCos ideally meet infrequently, and this is generally a waste of their time (most missed deadlines do not normally rise to the level where the SteerCo's involvement/decision is necessary). It also often puts the WL in an unfavorable light.

Note: if this is not the case in your organization, and your initiatives are in need of frequent SteerCo involvement, it could indicate structural issues with the initiative management foundation.

Pushback from pre-CRISP™ WLs who happen to hold management positions is not uncommon when it becomes necessary for them to step away from a critical path. They generally take this position: They feel *all* deliverables from their direct reports make them the de facto Producer.

While it is true they are ultimately accountable should there be issues, they are usually **not** directly responsible for the creation or procurement of needed Content. And by inserting themselves in the deliverable path, they disrupt not only the efficient flow of information, but can cause governance conflicts when/if things go wrong.

In addition to an increased workload, the most serious issue comes when a Producer who is a WL fails to deliver the NPC they are responsible for. While failed delivery is hopefully a rare occurrence, it creates a situation where the NP delivery escalation protocol is thwarted and a workaround must be instituted.

Of course, there is one instance where a Producer can be a Workstream Lead: when the WL *is* actually producing a deliverable needed by Consumers outside their Workstream. The escalation risk associated with this assignment should be brought to the attention of the SteerCo(s), so that if elevation becomes necessary, they are aware of the circumstances.

In these instances, the only escalation path available is to the SteerCo, and that is not ideal. And in a worst-case scenario where the WL/Producer is *also* a member of the SteerCo (yes, this happens more often than you would think), escalation may need to happen *outside* the Initiative to senior management organizationally accountable for the individual inhibiting progress.

For those situations where there is no other alternative because there just aren't enough people to go around, CRISP™ recommends doing the following:

1) Acknowledge the potential conflict up front when organizing and planning.
2) Clearly define a fast path to resolution with named individuals who have agreed to perform the role should issues arise.

3) Communicate the specific escalation terms to all potentially affected parties.

Recognizing (and addressing) this pattern early will help reduce the inevitable tension that occurs when things don't happen as expected.

Protocols and Process

Use and Importance

Achieving the levels of efficiency, effectiveness, and quality that CRISP™ provides is dependent on adherence to defined protocols and processes.

For clarity, in a business context, "protocol" and "process" both refer to structured approaches to achieve specific goals, but differ in flexibility and application. A "process" is a series of steps designed to accomplish a task, such as a due diligence review of accounting data. Processes under CRISP™ provide a flexible framework that can adapt to feedback and changing conditions, ensuring efficiency and consistency in operations.

A "protocol," however, is a set of strict rules that must be adhered to, especially in situations requiring compliance and coordination. Under CRISP™, protocols govern the specific behaviors associated with cross-functional and cross-entity communication, expressed through Key Artifacts and events, as well as the underlying concepts CRISP™ is based on. Unlike processes, protocols are intentionally rigid and leave little room for deviation, emphasizing the need for adherence to avoid risks and ensure compliance.

To summarize: processes guide ongoing activities with room for adaptation, while protocols enforce strict adherence to predefined rules. Both are crucial for maintaining order and compliance in complex scenarios like M&A.

Governance Organization

CRISP™ uses a device called a "Tactical Field Guide" (TFG) to organize protocols and processes into simple-to-use instructions. Similar in purpose to a "playbook," TFGs contain explicit rules for populating or editing Key Artifacts, scheduling and facilitating Consumer-Producer Review sessions, and more.

TFGs and their attendant protocols and processes are organized into three major categories necessary to operate CRISP™ once implemented.

1. Governance
2. Artifacts
3. Events

The Governance category contains TFGs for roles and responsibilities, as well as rules for how escalations are initiated and handled.

The Artifact category includes separate TFGs for each Key Artifact, as well as additional, optional "helper" artifacts, like the TSA Change Request form or standardized agenda model.

And finally, the Event category provides TFGs for each Key Event, plus examples and specific references for email messaging and related Colleague presentations used to support the events.

Because organizations define processes and protocols using their internal policies, specific details of TFG content, beyond the occasional mention of a rule or constraint, are outside the scope of this book.

Legal Oversight of Pre-Close Information Flow

Governance leading up to formally closing the deal requires structured legal oversight of information flow. Antitrust, employment, and sector-specific regulations constrain the type and timing of disclosures that can occur before close. CRISP™ accommodates these constraints through clear ownership and controlled distribution of NPC content by Producers, while all NPX entries remain visible to all Colleagues.

Under CRISP™ Key Artifact protocols, Producers maintain full control of NPC distribution. The NPX serves as a shared map and repository of what content exists and who owns it. In some cases, access to sensitive information only occurs only when a Producer releases NPC content as a response to a direct request from a Consumer. Governance structures can and should direct Producers to route sensitive categories of NPC, such as pricing models, wage data, or future operating scenarios, through counsel before release if it is not already company policy.

Legal oversight gains a structural advantage from the NPX. Instead of searching across multiple trackers, file stores, or project plans, counsel can review the complete pre-close NPX in a single location, identify entries that imply sensitive subject matter, and work with Producers to define review requirements or additional boundaries. Since the NPX exclusively deals with CF/CE exchanges, typical noise from extraneous inter-function data/documents is eliminated. This capability represents a meaningful improvement over traditional approaches that rely on scattered documents and isolated workstream-specific tools.

Please note: anytime access to NPC content is gated by a Producer, whether that Producer sits in legal, HR, IT, or any other function, execution efficiency is affected. "Gating" in this context means access to the final deliverable is not directly available in any artifact and must be requested by the Consumer. Governance guidance should acknowledge this trade-off, recognizing that stronger control and reduced regulatory risk also carry a corresponding increase in cycle time between NPX visibility and NPC access.

Governance Summary

Stable governance is a prerequisite for efficient execution. In CRISP™, stability means clear roles, defined escalation paths, and consistently applied interaction protocols, not rigidity.

Two parallel layers anchor the structure: Workstreams and the Steering Committee. Workstreams align with existing reporting lines and house accountable Producers. Workstream Leaders negotiate, escalate, and enforce protocol discipline, but should not serve as Producers in order to preserve clean elevation paths.

The Steering Committee is intentionally narrow. Its purpose is negotiation, escalation resolution, and realignment, not routine reporting. Executive time is reserved for decisions that materially affect the Initiative's progress.

An Initiative Administrator enforces protocols, maintains artifact integrity, coordinates events, and manages escalation thresholds. Clear backing from senior leadership is essential. Defined escalation sequences ensure issues are surfaced and resolved quickly rather than allowed to drift.

Protocols and Tactical Field Guides codify how roles operate, how information moves, and how sensitive data is controlled.

With authority defined, escalation paths clear, and protocols established, the governance structure is complete. The focus now shifts to the Key Artifacts that operationalize this structure and make disciplined execution possible.

NOTES

Key Artifacts

Execution in complex, cross-functional initiatives fails not because people don't care, but because there's often no shared framework that makes their care actionable. CRISP™ addresses this with a core set of Key Artifacts: standardized, initiative-wide tools that make responsibility clear, communication explicit, and execution trackable.

These artifacts are the backbone of operational alignment. They capture the "who, what, when, how and sometimes why" in a format optimized for visibility and action across all involved entities. Each artifact is tightly structured to eliminate ambiguity, reduce delays, and prevent the breakdowns that occur when assumptions go untested.

All Key Artifacts have the following in common:

Optimized, Not Overbuilt

Each artifact is engineered for operational optimization:

- Specific metadata fields reduce room for interpretation.
- Entity-level distinctions are baked in to reflect multi-organization collaboration.
- Designed for clarity, not perfection; fields support actual workflows, not theoretical models.

There's no fluff or decoration; just what's needed to ensure that Producers and Consumers of initiative-critical information stay aligned under pressure.

Using Your Tools

CRISP™ artifacts are designed to be rendered directly within your organization's existing tech ecosystem, whether that's Excel, Google Sheets, SharePoint, Notion, Airtable, or a proprietary tool. This enables:

- Fast deployment with minimal IT dependency.
- Familiar user interfaces that accelerate adoption and reduce training needs.
- Secure access control using established governance frameworks.
- Easier export, filtering, and analysis using tools already in place.

Important note: Because the artifacts aren't tied to any specific software, they can be adopted incrementally and adjusted over time without disrupting momentum. This has important adoption consequences, especially for Colleagues who are juggling day jobs along with demands from the initiative.

Compatible With Execution Platforms

While CRISP™ artifacts are platform-agnostic by design, they can be rendered within structured M&A execution tools like DealRoom, SmartMerger, or Midaxo when desired. In these environments, the artifacts can leverage built-in features such as:

- Workflow automation
- Role-based access controls
- Audit trails
- Notification systems
- Reportable metrics

Organizations already using M&A platforms can map CRISP™ artifacts to existing schemas, enhancing execution rigor without requiring system overhauls. Also know that creating a detailed configuration plan for this type of mapping is offered as a CRISP™ licensed service.

THE EIGHT KEY ARTIFACTS

The following sections introduce the eight Key Artifacts that power CRISP™-enabled execution:

1. **Milestone Schedule.** Captures the initiative's legal time constraints and leadership aspirations.
2. **NPX (Nexus Point Exchange).** The central exchange for Nexus Points (NPs) and their Content (NPC).
3. **Colleague Roster.** An authoritative list of who is involved, their role, and their access permissions.
4. **Employee Matrix.** The list of individuals whose affiliations are changing.
5. **Application Matrix.** Systems impacted, including testing environments and ownership.

6. **Request Log.** Tracks structured requests across multiple Parties and Entities.
7. **TSA (Transition Services Agreement).** Outlines the transitional services needed to temporarily stand up and operate the new entity.
8. **KTR (Knowledge Transfer Repository).** Contains auditable and referenceable video and documentation content based on explicit Buyer requests.

Each artifact is explained in the pages that follow, with sample content and guidance on usage. Together, they create a durable operational surface capable of supporting even the most complex initiatives.

Contextual Use

It should be mentioned that not all initiatives require every artifact. For example:

- A straightforward asset purchase might not require an Employee Matrix if no employee movement is anticipated.
- A carve-out with TSA obligations will rely heavily on the TSA, but may not need an Application Matrix if no technology is being transferred.
- Internal reorganizations may not need a Request List.

To these ends, CRISP™ is structured, not rigid. Each artifact stands alone but works best when adopted as part of a cohesive framework. When used together, they provide a complete operational map for any initiative, tailored to the specifics of the deal or transformation at hand.

Note: only the 1st three Key Artifacts are always required for CRISP™. The remaining documents are employed depending on the nature of the initiative.

Milestone Schedule

Every initiative needs a drumbeat to set the cadence and pace. The Milestone Schedule is that drumbeat.

It is the single source of truth associated with overall Initiative timing. Its content is based exclusively on key cross-entity events derived from dates specified in the deal's legal documents. For instances where CRISP™ is being used end-to-end, the Schedule would contain deadlines that exist in the LOI or formation documents; things like due diligence item submission dates.

"Sub-milestones" (events/dates occurring within isolated Workstreams) are not needed at the initiative level and should not be included in the schedule. Put another way, specific events/dates having no relevance to your own work scope are considered noise and should be omitted.

Key data in the schedule minimally includes the following:

1. **Event description.** For example, "Due Diligence document submission completed."
2. **Event date.** When the event is expected to happen based on the previously agreed-upon documents.
3. **Special Note.** Any additional explanatory notes. For example, "Date specified is immovable due to governing regulations."

In cases where a specific deliverable is tied to a milestone, a corresponding NPX entry should be made and noted as part of the description.

https://crispmethod.com/milestone-schedule/?cm_id=omae

Nexus Point Exchange (NPX)

An aspirational goal of CRISP™ is to put any Colleague within three clicks of the data they need. An NPX rendered as a filterable and searchable spreadsheet can meet this objective.

The NPX is the centralized repository for all Nexus Point Content (NPC), including the literal content or links to its source. It is designed to serve as the single source of truth for all cross-functional/cross-entity (CF/CE) information required to execute the transition or integration.

Important Reminder: Nexus Points (NPs) are **exclusively** cross-functional and/or cross-entity, meaning that if you are in the Finance Workstream and you need something from one of your Finance co-workers, that does not rise to the level of an NP. NPs are only for information you need from **outside** your Workstream or Entity.

Reminder 2: There are no NPs without Consumers. This should be obvious: If no one is going to need what has been described, why would anyone do it? Yet in practice, just as project plans often include tasks with no one (or TBD) assigned, NPs are created all the time with no Producers or Consumers specified. This is noise to be clarified or removed by the IMO or equivalent.

Also, each NP has one (and only one) named Producer. For potential communications and recognized responsibility, a single individual must be named.

For Traditional Project/Program Managers

If you are familiar with the project management concept of a RACI matrix (Responsible-Accountable-Consulted-Informed), the NPX is **all** Responsibility and Accountability; Producers are responsible for the content, and Workstream Leads are accountable, should issues with Producer delivery commitments or Content quality arise. The Consulted aspect of the RACI model is not needed in the NPX, as communication between Producers and Consumers make up the bulk of cross-functional communication. And because the NPX is accessible to all Colleagues, the notion of Informed disappears. See the full RACI mapping in a later section.

How CRISP™ Handles Interim Status (Hint: It Doesn't)

Under CRISP™, an NP only relies on 2 dates in order to be relevant: the Promise Date and the Delivery Date. CRISP™ asserts that there is no practical value in tracking a start date or a calculated or stipulated duration. Nor is it necessary to attempt to define and capture interim status or completion values. Producers are free (and expected) to perform whatever is needed to deliver NP Content on or before the Promise Date they agree to with the Consumers who need it. Full stop.

This is not to say that specific existing protocols or processes Workstream Producers operate within might mandate additional administrative record-keeping or updating. But as far as CRISP™ and the Consumers are concerned, the only timing data from outside their Workstream they need are Milestone Schedule dates and the Promise Dates for the NPC they need.

Pre-Close Information Exchange and Counsel Review

Pre-close information exchange operates under legal and regulatory constraints that define what can be shared, when sharing is appropriate, and which categories of information require special handling. Competitively sensitive material, including pricing, compensation, and future operating intentions, frequently requires involvement from counsel to avoid inappropriate disclosures.

CRISP™ supports these constraints through Producer-controlled access to NP content (NPC). Every Colleague can view all NPX entries without restriction. Consumers signal interest by tagging a specific NPX record and then, if delivery access is restricted, contacting the Producer directly to request the related NPC. Producer ownership of NPC content keeps sensitive detail outside the NPX while still maintaining full transparency into what content exists.

Companies are encouraged to include counsel in the approval mix for any pre-close NPC that may create antitrust or regulatory exposure. Company policy can formalize this expectation so that legal review is consistently applied when required.

The NPX structure provides an additional benefit to legal teams that traditional approaches do not offer: counsel can review the entire set of NPX entries (pre and post close) in one place, identify potential high-risk items, and work with Producers to define appropriate distribution boundaries before any NPC is shared. This is an example of the High Fidelity Observation CRISP™ provides to any initiative.

Remember - anytime access to NPC content is gated by a Producer, including legal, HR, IT, or other functions responsible for sensitive material, some reduction in execution efficiency should be expected. Delivery must wait until the gate criteria are satisfied, which introduces time between initial interest in the NPX entry and actual access to the underlying NPC, assuming the content is available. In other words, make sure access restrictions are truly necessary so as not to introduce unneeded delays into the initiative.

For a literal look at a formerly active NPX and how it can be used, use this QR code or navigate to the URL below for a video of actual NPX usage, showing Consumer, Producer, and IMO use cases.

https://crispmethod.com/npx-demonstration?cm_id=omae

Colleague Roster

The Colleague Roster plays a vital role in maintaining clarity and alignment throughout an initiative. The deliberate use of the word **"Colleague"** is central to CRISP™.

The term reinforces equality of contribution across Buyer, Seller, and Advisor entities, regardless of title or organizational hierarchy. By framing every participant as a Colleague, CRISP™ eliminates the unhelpful barriers that arise when individuals are labeled by role alone or ambiguous group. It emphasizes that success depends on mutual accountability, shared respect, and precision in communication.

Why "Colleague" Matters

Choosing "Colleague" over alternatives such as "resource," "employee," or "team member" is intentional. Each of those terms carries baggage:

- **Resource** reduces individuals to interchangeable inputs.
- **Employee** narrows scope to one side of the deal and excludes external advisors.
- **Team member** implies bounded groups, which is at odds with the cross-functional, cross-entity, peer-to-peer communication CRISP™ enables.

Colleague is universal. It applies equally to participants in both organizations and to third parties. It captures the spirit of cooperation that initiatives demand.

Benefits of a Single Standardized Source of Truth

The Colleague Roster acts as the single, standardized source of truth for all people involved in the initiative. Without it, individual workstreams and individuals often maintain separate, inconsistent lists of participants. That inconsistency inherently creates noise and leads to confusion. With one roster in place:

- **Consistency across Workstreams:** Everyone references the same roster, eliminating duplication and misalignment.
- **Faster onboarding:** New participants quickly know who else is engaged and where to direct questions.
- **Clarity of accountability:** Producers and Consumers can be clearly tied to deliverables.
- **Reduced noise:** Outdated or conflicting contact information is removed from circulation.
- **Alignment across entities:** Buyer, Seller, and Advisors can coordinate using shared data rather than isolated views.

Metadata Captured in the Colleague Roster

Beyond basic names and contact information, the Colleague Roster captures essential metadata that supports execution precision:

- **Role.** Defines the function the Colleague performs in the initiative, not just their job title.
- **Workstream affiliation.** Identifies where their contributions fit within the initiative's structure.
- **Security access level.** Ensures that the right Colleagues have the appropriate level of access to sensitive data.
- **Entity alignment.** Distinguishes whether the Colleague is part of the Buyer, Seller, or Advisor group.

By maintaining this structured metadata in a single artifact, CRISP™ creates clarity in ownership, purpose, and timing. Dependencies are understood, messaging behavior is agreed to, and everyone can focus on delivering what is needed, when it is needed.

https://crispmethod.com/colleague-roster/?cm_id=omae

Employee Matrix

Definition and Scope

The Employee Matrix lists non-colleague employees scheduled to transition as part of the initiative, including employees transferring, separating, or remaining under Transitional Services Agreement coverage. The Employee Matrix exists to support clear decisions about offers, timing, access, provisioning, and on/offboarding activities that affect transitioning employees.

Boundary With the Colleague Roster

The Colleague Roster lists Initiative Colleagues from Buyer, Seller, and Advisors who directly participate in planning and execution. The Colleague Roster does not typically include transitioning employees who are not performing initiative roles outside their day-to-day jobs.

That said, occasional overlap can occur. An individual can appear as a Colleague in the Colleague Roster and separately as a transitioning employee in the Employee Matrix. The Colleague Roster records collaboration attributes for initiative work. The Employee Matrix records transition attributes for employment change. The distinction must remain explicit in field names, views, and governance.

Single Source of Truth

The Employee Matrix functions as a single standardized source of truth. One document, one location, one agreed structure. All changes follow a controlled update path with visible ownership and auditable history.

Who Needs Access, and When?

Access requirements extend well beyond Human Resources and change as the initiative progresses.

- **Corporate Development and Deal Team** during diligence and sign-to-close: counts by function and location, employment classifications, union and works council flags, leadership mapping, retention candidates, and regulatory constraints.
- **Integration Management Office** across planning and cutover: alignment of headcount to deliverables, Day 1 readiness, interim role coverage, and stabilization checkpoints.
- **Functional Leaders** across all workstreams: confirmation of who transitions, when transitions occur, and what capability coverage exists at each Milestone.
- **Finance** through modeling and close: cost baselines, retention commitments, severance projections, and synergy realization tracking tied to headcount moves.
- **Legal and Compliance** throughout: entity transfers, offer mechanics, notification requirements, restrictive covenants, immigration and visa considerations, and records retention.
- **IT** pre-close through Day 1 and stabilization: identity creation, role-based access, license rationalization, application and network provisioning and de-provisioning, and device handover plans.
- **Security and Facilities** for cutover: badge issuance, site access, escort requirements, asset return, and physical occupancy changes.
- **Payroll and Benefits** for Day 1 readiness: pay cycle alignment, banking validation checkpoints, benefits election windows, and COBRA or regional equivalents.
- **Communications** for timing and content: audience counts, leader lists, site rollups, and sequencing for announcements.

Core Data Schema

The Employee Matrix remains lean yet sufficient for most uses not requiring PII (Personally Identifiable Information). Typical fields include:

- Unique employee identifier, prior system identifier, and person-level deduplication key
- Legal name and preferred name
- Function, role title, and Workstream alignment for capability mapping
- Current entity, future entity, site or location, and employment type
- Classification markers such as exempt status, union membership, or works council applicability
- Manager name and manager mapping post-close
- Transition category such as transfer, retain at Seller under TSA, or separation
- Effective dates for offer, transfer, separation, and access changes
- Retention program indicator and program end date
- Regulatory or immigration flags and required actions
- Application access footprint summarized to application families for planning
- Physical asset footprint summary for device and badge handling
- Data classification level to drive distribution controls

Sensitive fields remain minimized. Deep PII such as national identifiers, full birthdates, and bank details remain stored only in the HR system of record. The recommended way of managing Employee Matrix PII references is through governed keys managed by the Employee Data Handler.

Governance and Controls

Strong governance protects accuracy, compliance, and trust.

- **Ownership.** Named HR data owner, named IMO data steward (in CRISP™ this is called the Employee Data Handler), and optionally, named Legal compliance reviewer.
- **Change control.** Defined request channel, explicit approver list, timestamped change log, and reason codes.
- **Versioning.** Immutable snapshots at key Milestones and cutover gates, with labeled baseline and delta views.
- **Access.** Least-privilege role model, read-only distribution for non-owners, and watermarked extracts where extracts remain unavoidable.
- **Quality checks.** Scheduled validations for duplicates, missing managers, date conflicts, and entity mismatches.
- **Privacy.** Field-level masking for broad audiences, segregated storage for any high-sensitivity attributes, and retention rules aligned to jurisdictional requirements.

Operating Conventions

- **No personal copies.** Use governed views or controlled extracts with expiration.

- **No uncontrolled columns.** Extend the schema only through change control.
- **No mixed purposes.** Keep collaboration attributes in the Colleague Roster and transition attributes in the Employee Matrix.
- **No silent edits.** Record every change with owner, reason, and timestamp.

Common Failure Modes and CRISP™ Guardrails

- **Shadow files** create divergent truths. Guardrail: read-only views and watermarked extracts with expiry.
- **Role confusion** merges Colleague and transitioning-employee attributes. Guardrail: explicit field names and separate artifact links from every downstream view.
- **Privacy drift** exposes high-sensitivity data. Guardrail: minimal fields, masking, and strict access roles.
- **Date incoherence** breaks cutover plans. Guardrail: automated validations for effective dates and entity changes tied to Milestone gates.

The Employee Matrix, governed as a single source of truth and separated from the Colleague Roster by clear boundaries, enables accurate planning, clean Day 1 execution, and compliant stabilization across Buyer, Seller, and Advisor entities. Strict governance, disciplined access, and field-lean design sustain confidence in every decision that relies on the Employee Matrix.

https://crispmethod.com/employee-matrix/?cm_id=omae

Application Matrix

The **Application Matrix** serves as the single source of truth for all software applications impacted by an initiative. It documents current and future state usage, dependencies, and responsibilities, ensuring clarity and governance across Buyers, Sellers, and Advisors.

Unlike the Employee Matrix, which is focused only on transitioning individuals, the Application Matrix captures the systems environment that underpins day-to-day operations and the future state. Because application portfolios are often complex and fragmented across entities, a tightly governed Application Matrix is essential for avoiding misaligned assumptions, duplicate system build-outs, and costly post-close surprises.

Purpose and Scope

The Application Matrix provides a consolidated record of:

- All applications in scope for the initiative.
- Their owners/admins and primary functions.
- Current and future usage across entities.
- Testing, integration, training, and cut-over needs.
- Key dates and dependencies tied to initiative milestones.

It ensures that decisions about application retention, replacement, or integration are made with full visibility and consensus.

Governance and Access

Strict governance of the Application Matrix is mandatory. Multiple contributors, beyond IT, require access at different times, including:

- **Business Unit Leaders**, to validate usage and dependencies.
- **Finance and Operations**, to ensure cost alignment and budgeting for licenses or replacements.
- **Security and Compliance**, to confirm risk, data integrity, and regulatory requirements.
- **Integration Management Office (IMO)**, to track alignment with initiative milestones and confirm cutover plans.

To maintain integrity, the Application Matrix document should always be maintained as the **single source of truth**, with updates controlled by designated owners.

Key Elements

The artifact typically includes:

- **Application Name.** The system or platform under review.
- **Product Owner.** Accountable for business decisions related to the application.
- **Function ("What it Does").** Description of its business purpose.
- **Current and Future Usage.** Whether the application is actively used now, will continue post-close, or is planned for retirement.
- **Instances.** Details on whether new environments are needed or existing ones will be retained.

- **Testing, Training, and Cutover.** Requirements for test environments, training needs, timing of shutdown/go-live, and validation of dependencies.
- **Integrations.** Both active and required integrations to be established or maintained.
- **Key Dates.** Readiness for testing, training, go-live dates, and related milestones.
- **Notes.** Clarifying details, open questions, or entity-specific considerations.

Additional properties like user counts should be added as needed.

Importance

The Application Matrix is critical because it:

- Provides transparency into the systems landscape.
- Reduces risk of missed dependencies or unbudgeted license costs.
- Aligns technical and business stakeholders on application decisions.
- Ensures initiative cutover and Day-1 readiness by embedding dependencies into timing and ownership.

https://crispmethod.com/application-matrix/?cm_id=omae

Request List

The **Request List** is the governing artifact for managing cross-entity requests during an initiative. It functions as the single source of truth for Buyer–Seller interactions, capturing, tracking, and reconciling all requests that pass between entities and their contributors. While Workstreams may maintain their own internal processes to manage day-to-day activity, the Request List ensures that enterprise-level coordination remains transparent, auditable, and tightly governed.

Purpose and Scope

The Request List exists to:

- Centralize all CF/CE initiative-related requests into one controlled environment.
- Enable both Buyer and Seller to view, validate, and act upon requests without duplication.
- Provide a consistent format for capturing request details, ownership, timing, and resolution status.
- Embed accountability by recording criticality, dates needed, and responsible individuals across entities.
- Ensure every request is linked directly to a specific NPX or TSA line item. No "general" or unaligned requests are permitted.

Structure of the Request List

Each row represents a single request and contains standardized fields, including:

- **Request ID/RefID.** The unique identifiers for traceability. RefID is mandatory and must map to a specific NPX or TSA entry.
- **Request Type.** A coded classification with controlled values:

- Knowledge Transfer
- SME Meeting
- Change—Process
- Change—Config
- Other

- **Shortname.** A descriptive nickname for the item (e.g., *"App license agreement"*).
- **Request Description.** Clear articulation of what is being asked for.
- **Criticality and Date Needed.** This establishes urgency and the expected delivery window.
- **Status Fields.** Separate Buyer and Seller perspectives with values drawn from a controlled list:
  - Submitted
  - Received
  - Under Review
  - In Progress
  - Rejected
  - Canceled
  - Complete
- **Contacts and SMEs.** Named individuals for ownership and accountability.
- **Assignment.** A record of who has responsibility for fulfillment.
- **Associated Files.** A reference to linked or supporting documents.

- **Audit Metadata.** Automatically captured creation and modification details (time and author).

This structure ensures that requests are tracked from inception through resolution, with complete visibility into timing, responsibility, and supporting evidence.

Lookup Tables (LUTs)

When rendered in spreadsheet form, a **LUTs** sheet standardizes key inputs to the Request List by providing controlled vocabularies for request types, departments, and Workstream abbreviations. This prevents classification ambiguity and guarantees consistent reporting across the initiative.

Governance

IA Colleagues from both the Buyer and the Seller are responsible for grooming the list: conferring with affected Colleagues, checking for duplicates, ensuring dates align with deliverable schedules, updating IA fields, and resolving discrepancies. Their role ensures the artifact remains clean, reliable, and directly connected to initiative-level deliverables.

> **Caution**: **When following CRISP™ protocols,** informal requests that are **not** recorded in the Request List have **zero support from the IMO**. That means if such a request goes unfulfilled, there is no predetermined escalation path to resolve the issue, causing any number of unplanned interruptions and interventions. This type of activity (informal, back-channel requests) is common during carve-outs or divestitures, increases in frequency as milestones are approached, and, for obvious reasons, should be strongly discouraged.

Key Benefits

- **Transparency:** Both Buyer and Seller share visibility into outstanding and completed requests.

- **Accountability:** Named owners and SMEs eliminate ambiguity in responsibility.
- **Control:** Controlled vocabularies and metadata lock in consistency.
- **Auditability:** Full change history, including creation and modification tracking.
- **Alignment:** Ensures every request is anchored to a deliverable in the NPX or TSA, preventing noise and misdirection.

Relation to NPX and TSA

The Request List is used only when a structured, cross-entity request must be tracked and managed. The Request List does not duplicate the NPX or TSA. **In all cases, Request List entries require a TSA or NPX reference.** If the request can't be tied back to a specific existing deliverable, either a reference deliverable (NPX or TSA) must be created or the request should be escalated, as it could very well be outside the scope of the initiative.

https://crispmethod.com/request-list/?cm_id=omae

TSA (Transition Service Agreement) Matrix

The Transition Service Agreement (TSA) Matrix is an optional artifact within CRISP™, used typically when the Buyer requires continued support from the Seller for a defined period following close. Not every initiative requires a TSA, but when it does, this artifact provides a structured, single source of truth for the services to be delivered, their costs, and their operational implications.

Since legal teams, in conjunction with their functional SMEs, determine the content, boundaries, and final version of the TSA, the following recommendations for the structure of the worksheet must be vetted and approved by both parties prior to adoption.

Each TSA item is cataloged in a worksheet by **reference number, Workstream, sub-Workstream, description, duration, cost elements, methodology, and interdependency notes**. The reference numbering follows a consistent schema: base operational items are numbered in sequence, while **transition or wind-down activities are designated by adding a suffix to the related operational item reference number**. This allows initiative leaders to quickly identify which services are essential for day-one continuity and which represent phase-out obligations.

Because TSA services are negotiated between Buyer and Seller, the document must remain flexible. **Changes to TSA items are expected during the artifact's lifetime.** The Tactical Field Guide (TFG) for handling TSAs provides explicit procedures for submitting and reviewing a **TSA Change Form**, which documents modifications to scope, duration, or cost. This ensures consistency and traceability across all TSA-related adjustments.

As previously mentioned, working with legal is essential in keeping the TSA structure **friendly to initiative execution**. Put another way, agreements that ignore the practical implications of what they represent do not provide clarity. Overly rigid service definitions or unnecessarily complicated termination clauses can undermine the ability of executives and Workstream Leaders to manage operations effectively. Legal teams should be guided to prioritize:

- **Clarity of deliverables** without excessive administrative burden.
- **Defined escalation paths** that align with initiative governance.
- **Reasonable flexibility** in service duration and cost adjustments to reflect the evolving nature of integration.
- **Simplicity in language**, so that the artifact can be understood by both executives negotiating the agreement and Workstream Leaders responsible for execution.

The TSA artifact stands alone but also **touches other CRISP™ artifacts**. TSA milestones often appear in the **Milestone Schedule**, and dependencies embedded in TSA items may be visible in the **Request List** or NPX, where Producers and Consumers need to align. However, TSA items are managed as a distinct body of work given their contractual and financial implications.

For **initiative executives**, the TSA provides a negotiation baseline and a risk-management instrument, ensuring continuity of service while controlling exposure to cost overruns. For **Workstream leaders (and the IMO)**, the TSA is a daily operating reference, defining what support is available, for how long, and at what cost. By maintaining strict governance of this artifact, CRISP™ ensures that TSA services, while temporary, are executed with the same discipline as permanent deliverables.

Given the nature of the TSA, it is recommended that updated versions be available at a predetermined cadence, in conjunction with the agreed-upon billing interval (monthly is recommended). This practice allows invoices to be generated in sync with changes to TSA line items, simplifying auditing or identifying discrepancies.

IMPORTANT NOTE: TSA schedules are legal instruments regularly created in Excel and rendered and distributed as part of a PDF document. To be useful, the IMO needs access to the original spreadsheet or an OCR data conversion to facilitate ongoing maintenance. Otherwise, cutting and pasting into a new spreadsheet is the only way to operationalize the data.

https://crispmethod.com/transition-services-agreement-matrix/?cm_id=omae

Knowledge Transfer Repository (KTR)

While the KTR is not technically a Key Artifact, a brief discussion of its design and use is included here as it serves as a single point of truth for all Knowledge Transfer artifacts.

KTR's are usually created as a separate area within the managed storage space the Initiative uses. This simplifies access management for the IA and Colleagues. For consistency, the underlying folder structure should emulate the Workstream structures, so that saving and locating transferred knowledge artifacts is obvious and straight forward.

It's very important a uniform file naming convention be established to quickly identify the subject matter without needing to inspect artifact content. Since all KT is driven by formal requests and is tracked against specific TSA items, folders should match each TSA schedule identifier. Filenames should also begin with TSA identifier and include the subject of the artifact and the date the artifact was created. Here is an example of what that looks like:

Finance > FIN_04 > FIN-04_Payroll-KT-20250312.mp4

"Finance" is a top-level folder, "FIN_04" is a sub-folder mapped to the required TSA schedule item identifier, and the filename explicitly names the TSA identifier ("Fin_04"), the subject matter ("Payroll-KT"), and the date the artifact was created ("20250312"). Note: In some cases there may be only 1 artifact in the subfolder, but often there will be many.

Last, it's critical that all KT artifacts are stored as view-only documents to protect their integrity from alteration.

Following this basic design ensures the results of KT are easy to find for real-time use by Colleagues and any post-KT auditing that may be required. In addition, once completed the entire KTR can easily be copied to the Buyer's protected environment for use after the transition is finished.

https://crispmethod.com/ktr/?cm_id=omae

"Helper" Artifacts

Not all of the 8 Key Artifacts are applicable to every initiative, and the same is true of CRISP™'s Helper Artifacts. However, they can be particularly useful in specific situations.

Standardized Agendas for Issue Tracing

Imagine a scenario where you are trying to understand who, what, where, when, why, and how a specific decision was made that materially affected the Initiative—a chain-of-custody for the decision. This is a common occurrence at the SteerCo level when CF/CE disputes are escalated to the executives for disposition and decisions made during the meetings fail to get communicated to the proper parties and then reappear days, weeks or months later. While many templates exist for recording agendas and minutes, their focus is primarily on a single event rather than a collection of events.

Standardized agendas and contemporaneous notes (or recordings), on the other hand, formatted in a time-series and stored in known, accessible locations or systems, allow searchable archives for easily conducting Initiative-related discovery without resorting to using AI or outboard search mechanisms. Typically, these agendas would be stored/cataloged by Workstream, with SME-specific agendas in SME-specific folders or areas. IMO, SteerCo, WL, and Initiative-level agendas following the same format should be used as well.

If your collaboration tool supports this kind of feature, the TFG offers ways to configure it. If not, a simple solution is to use a spreadsheet, with each meeting recorded as a separate tab/sheet, to provide a single, time-series document that can be easily managed and searched. The CRISP™ Agenda artifact also provides a model that includes automatic line-item timeboxing to ensure topics receive adequate time within the constraints of the overall meeting.

From the CRISP™ perspective, agendas and other project artifacts need to ostensibly be in one place for ease of access. See the Technology platform prep chapter for recommended deployment designs with collaboration tools and shared-storage solutions.

https://crispmethod.com/standardized-agenda/?cm_id=omae

TSA Change Request Form

Direct interaction between initiative IAs with respect to handling TSA changes is a continuing activity that requires consistency to avoid confusion and duplicated effort. To make that activity easy and precise, each change should be documented with a CRISP™ Change Request (CR), which is represented by a form.

The CR form captures the specific information needed to vet and implement the change, and its TFG describes the required approval messaging needed for post-change audit or discovery actions. See the TSA Administration section for a detailed explanation.

https://crispmethod.com/tsa-change-request/?cm_id=omae

Countdown Reminder

As either an add on to the Milestone artifact or as a graphic sent by email, the Countdown Reminder keeps the reality of critical event dates front and center by including how many work and calendar days remain until the target date arrives.

In most cases the Countdown reminder is created, published and managed by the IA with input from WLs as to what items to include and their associated dates. But the same artifact can also be used by individual Workstreams for their internal functional alignment.

The example below was used to highlight key dates related to specific TSA items.

https://crispmethod.com/countdown-reminder/?cm_id=omae

NOTES

KEY EVENTS

Over the course of an initiative, key events happen. Some are attached to milestones, but many are not.

By design, there are a small number of key events required to get the full level of efficiency and effectiveness out of CRISP™. This chapter describes the events, how they are structured, the prerequisites needed, and potential obstacles you may encounter when scheduling, staging, or executing them.

OVERVIEW

This chapter starts with a review of the phases or segments of a CRISP™ initiative. Then onto specific events (or "ceremonies" in some parlance). There are three major periods:

1) Preparation
2) Execution
3) Transition

The periods are further broken down by phases. In the Preparation Period, there are five primary events required by CRISP™; they are in sequence:

- Populating the NPX
- Individual review by both Consumers and Producers
- Producer-Consumer NP/NPC vetting
- Initiative-wide alignment (two sessions)
- Initiative-wide readiness (one session)

Events defined as regularly cadenced meetings come next; there are a minimum of two at the Initiative level for each entity:

1) Steering committees (Buyer and Seller)
2) Workstream leads (Buyer and Seller)

It's important to note that for **all** events, CRISP™ actively avoids the highly inefficient practice of reporting on general "status." The reason for this is straightforward: Since NP Producers and their Consumers (where the actual work happens) agree on delivery details, and since those details have timing or dependency dates built in, the necessity to review the status of work underway, especially in a group setting, like a SteerCo or WL meeting, is unnecessary and wastes people's time.

This is not to say that WLs should not interact with the Producers they are accountable for; far from it. The CRISP™ rule is that when Producers miss their commitments (and they will), it immediately triggers escalation to the appropriate WL for disposition. And since everyone can see in the NPX what (and who) is late, the focus of group interaction is to shine a light on the responsible Producers (and their accountable WLs) to put peer or, if necessary, organizational pressure to achieve a resolution.

Last, CRISP™ recommends expanding and applying the "Law of Two Feet" in non-compulsory meetings. Developed by Harrison Owen in 1985, the principle suggests that if participants in a meeting find themselves in a situation where they are neither learning nor contributing, they should use their "two feet" to move to a place where they can be more productive. In today's context, "move to a place" should also be interpreted as "drop off the call." This "law" empowers individuals to take responsibility for their participation and, when used appropriately, can free up time for Colleagues to spend on more productive things.

Foundational Initiative Phases

In CRISP™, every initiative progresses through three major periods: **Preparation, Execution, and Transition**. Each period is divided into structured phases that establish ownership, timing, and deliverable alignment. While the framework is consistent, the contents and duration of each phase vary depending on the type of initiative; a spin-off has different requirements than an acquisition or carve-out.

1. Preparation Period

The Preparation Period begins once leadership decides to move forward and ends with a kick-off. Preliminary activities such as due diligence, market research, and shareholder alignment may span many months or years; however, once the Go Signal is given, CRISP™ compresses the Preparation Period into less than 2.5 months.

https://crispmethod.com/preparation-period/?cm_id=omae

Phases of Preparation Period

1. **Set-up and Introduction (≈10 days).** The initiative environment is established; governance is defined; tools and protocols are put in place; and top-level team alignment is secured. These steps create a single foundation for execution. This is also when the NPX is populated, and the Milestone Schedule is set.
2. **Independent Reviews (5–10 days).** Producers and Consumers independently review NPX items; deliverable packages are refined; ownership and context are confirmed; Producers validate readiness for collaboration. This is also known as the Individual Vetting process.
3. **Collaboration Sessions (15–20 days).** Producers and Consumers engage in IMO-facilitated and sequenced structured negotiation/validation sessions; NPX deliverables are reviewed; promise dates are acknowledged, renegotiated, or escalated; and sequencing dependencies are surfaced. The outcome is a shared understanding of all Nexus Points across entities and functions at a granular level between the specific Colleagues responsible for producing and consuming the content. This is also known as the Consumer-Producer Nexus Point Vetting process.
4. **Readiness Sessions (15–20 days).** Milestone sequencing is confirmed; final adjustments are negotiated; and readiness is validated across all Workstreams. The Preparation Period concludes with "Kick-off," which functions as a handoff rather than a ceremonial event.

2. Execution Period

https://crispmethod.com/execution-period/?cm_id=omae

The Execution Period represents the **Run Mode** of the initiative. It encompasses all activities required to accommodate the initiative up to and including the go-live dates. The length of this period is highly variable; some initiatives move rapidly to a conclusion, while others require sustained operation over months or years.

Phase of Execution Period

- **Run Mode.** Execution advances as deliverables are produced and validated. Workstream activity centers on fulfilling commitments defined in the NPX, milestones are met through negotiated delivery, and progress is continuously visible to leadership. Noise is monitored and reduced, with issues surfaced and resolved in real time. Execution continues until transition signals indicate readiness to hand over responsibility.

3. Transition Period

https://crispmethod.com/transition-period/?cm_id=omae

The Transition Period begins once execution signals the handover point. It covers all activities required to meet post–go-live needs and to formally conclude initiative responsibilities. For some initiatives, this includes executing **Transition Service Agreements (TSAs)**, which are optional but frequently used in spin-offs and carve-outs. For acquisitions or mergers, this is where Integration happens.

Phases of the Transition Period

1. **Transition.** Operational handover is the focus; accountability moves from initiative Workstreams to ongoing business units; knowledge transfer is completed. Where TSAs exist, they are executed to provide temporary continuity. The scope of Transition varies significantly; a carve-out may rely heavily on TSA provisions, while an acquisition may require a more integration-focused handover.

2. **Close.** Closure finalizes the initiative; deliverables are verified; remaining obligations are addressed; TSA amendments are processed if required. Workstreams wind down at different times depending on their role, but all conclude with a formal sign-off. Lessons learned are documented and archived to inform future initiatives.

Notes on Variation

The framework applies universally; however, the scope and timing of each phase differ depending on initiative type and context. Carve-outs emphasize TSA execution, acquisitions emphasize integration deliverables, and joint ventures or mergers may emphasize extended Run Mode. CRISP™ provides a disciplined model that adapts to these differences without losing clarity or accountability.

NPX Data Population

The initial population of the NPX is one of, if not the, most critical aspect of CRISP™.

The first time it is performed is the hardest. Since the data can and should be used going forward, subsequent NPX population exercises, regardless of transaction type, get significantly easier and much faster to do as they build on the existing NPs. And for organizations with dedicated teams, the ability to obtain high-fidelity observation across all active and inactive initiatives provides a perspective that is very difficult to achieve, even with special-purpose applications.

While NPX Data Population is described as a single event, it is actually comprised of several steps conducted by multiple Colleagues. The basic steps for the initial build are straightforward:

1. From all Workstreams, collect or access any historical artifacts used to identify data that is needed in the course of the Initiative.
    a. Typically, this data can be found in requirements documents and standardized forms and checklists.
    b. Note on forms: NPs can (and should) contain links to forms that serve as single deliverables. An example of this would be a Finance-related form asking for labels from Operations for new GL accounting codes.

c. If you are fortunate enough to have an active and robust Master Data Management program in use, it is possible that 80% or more of the data you need could come from that source.

d. TIP: Creating an indexed catalog of source material that can be referenced back to individual NPs later for quality purposes is highly recommended. Taking this step provides a backstop to questions that Colleagues invariably ask during the vetting process, i.e., "Where did this NP come from?"

2. Load the NPX with the relevant Nexus Points.

    a. Remember that NPs must be unique and unambiguous, and **must** be required by one or more Workstream Consumers. NPs without Consumers represent unneeded work.

    b. While each NP is associated with the Producer's Workstream, the NPX is **not** a repository for items that are strictly used **within** a single Workstream.

    c. **TIP**: As mentioned in the step above, including a source material reference ID during this step will prove invaluable for the next step and answering the question "Is this a CF/ CE NP?"

3. Each NP must be tested by the IMO for each of the following attributes:

    a. It must be CF/CE data or information, meaning that a Workstream SME must need data from **outside** of their Workstream or Entity.

    b. It must be unique. Duplicates violate a "single-source-of-truth" constraint, create confusion and delay, and add cost if changes are made and synchronization is lost. The NPX allows and encourages the callout of synonyms within its structure to assist with navigation and search, as different Workstreams and Entities often have different names for the same thing.

c. It must have a single, responsible Producer. The Content connected with an NP (the NPC) comes from somewhere, and that somewhere must resolve to the individual who is responsible for delivering the NPC. Indirect "Producership," where the actual resources doing the work are different than who is responsible for delivery, is only allowed if the Producer directly represents and participates in the team charged with producing the NPC. For reasons mentioned elsewhere, hierarchical Producership (Producers whose connection to the Content is based purely on reporting or org structure, not active creation tasks) is strongly discouraged as it introduces unavoidable Hierarchical Filtering and Governance issues.

While every Initiative is different, the actual number of NPs will be generally less than 500 for start-to-finish coverage. If the NPX is used only for post-close execution, the number of NPs drops to around 300. "Mileage" will vary, of course, depending on the complexity of the initiative (how many Parties/Entities), the environments (source and target), and the level of granularity needed.

Once the initial population is complete, the NPX must be published and made available for all Colleagues to **individually** weigh in. CRISP™ defines this time-boxed activity as the Individual Vetting Period (IVP).

> Note: Field experience has shown that "complete" in this regard is rarely 100%. But due to CRISP™'s design, any completion above 60% can achieve success, with rates at 80% or higher virtually guaranteed to get the initiative over the finish line in record time.

During this review process, Consumers, at their convenience but before a hard deadline, fill in any gaps, tag the NPs they need, and correct any errors that occur during the population process.

Producers do a similar review, looking specifically at the NPC description, whether they are the proper source for delivering the NPC, and ideally, when that delivery might be, given their current workload and the Initiative Milestones. If the input of promised delivery dates is collected during this step, it will save precious time during the next step.

TIP: While not required, it is recommended to sequence the IVP with the Producers review happening first, quickly followed by the Consumers. Sequencing like this has a couple of benefits that help Colleagues and the IMO:

1) Producers can flag those NPs that have been erroneously assigned to them so that the true Producer can be established.
2) When the Producers specify their Promise Dates ahead of the Consumer IVP, the recognition of those dates, relative to Milestones, provides an additional feedback point for Consumers. This could allow Consumers to skip the consensus sessions (reducing their initiative time burden) if they are satisfied with the date the Producer is promising, relative to their work.

Producer-Consumer NP Consensus Sessions

The Producer-Consumer relationship is the fulcrum of CRISP™, and it's easy to understand why: It's the fundamental component needed to ensure things get done on time and to the satisfaction of all Colleagues. The first formal recognition of this relationship is the NP consensus sessions.

After the deadline to populate and vet the NPX, which includes Consumers tagging or creating all the NPC references they need, a formalized review of each Producer's NPs with the Consumers is performed.

The IMO schedules and facilitates these key events to ensure they are conducted and complete, and to immediately catch any disconnects or potential escalation issues. They should be sequenced in priority order, based on the Impact Score calculated for each Producer.

Impact Scores

Impact Scores are calculated for each NP by summing the number of Workstreams that have expressed an interest in that NP. Producer Impact Scores are the sum of NP scores for their individual deliverables. This list can easily be extracted from the NPX after the deadline to populate it has been reached, and then when needed throughout the initiative. Here's an example of what that looks like:

https://crispmethod.com/impact-score-calculation/?cm_id=omae

Explanation: NPX-0106's score is 1, 0109's score is 3. (The Producer's Workstream is never used in the calculation.) If these were the only two NPs that Glaw Uozpkv was responsible for, their Producer impact score would be 4.

Calculating impact scores has the following benefits:

1) Potential bottlenecks caused by Producers who are overloaded can be easily spotted.
2) Prioritization of NP Producer-Consumer reviews becomes automatic as Producers with higher impact scores naturally have NPs that

have a greater need, influenced by the number of Consumer Workstreams.

3) Likewise, NP Impact Scores give a similar, relative ranking, allowing the IMO to quickly segregate low-impact NPs (where only one or two Workstreams are in need of the Content) from high-impact NPs (where potentially all Workstreams need the Content).

Session Format

Facilitated by a member of the IMO (ideally, the IA conducts the high-priority sessions), a group consisting of the Producer and the Consumers who need content from the Producer, reviews **each** assigned NP and minimally agrees on these things:

1) That the correct Producer is associated with the NP
2) What the NP Content is and how it will be delivered
3) The date on which the NPC is to be delivered

The facilitator makes any proposed changes, notes any future action (like finding a new Producer or escalating timing disagreements), and moves to the next NP. For efficiency, these sessions should be timeboxed. Use three minutes per NP as the metric.

Law of Two Feet applicable? Yes. Consumers who have prior, trusted working relationships with Producers where they have previously received similar or the same deliverables are allowed to skip these sessions, **provided** they have reviewed the current promise dates and they align with their needs.

STEERING COMMITTEE SESSIONS

As previously mentioned, unlike traditional governance bodies that often become forums for updates and reporting, a CRISP™ SteerCo exists solely to address escalated issues and enable direct interaction among executive-level Colleagues across entities and between functions.

For any initiative involving a Buyer and Seller, three SteerCos need to be established:

Entity-Specific SteerCos. Internal to each Buyer or Seller organization, these bodies resolve escalations that can be settled without joint discussion. They serve as the first line of executive-level decision-making.

Joint SteerCo. Comprised of senior Colleagues from both entities, this body convenes when escalations span organizational boundaries or when alignment at the highest level is required.

Where an initiative is "self-contained" (no Buyer or Seller, i.e., a spin-off), only one SteerCo is needed. Optionally, if the size and scope warrant a large number of advisors or consultants, a Joint SteerCo should be created to function as a supplier-focused body.

To minimize executive involvement, cadence is also intentionally limited. Regularly scheduled SteerCo meetings should not occur more than bi-weekly, and when the initiative is progressing smoothly with few escalations, a monthly cadence is preferable. This reflects their unique nature: they are the most expensive meetings in terms of Colleague time, with the narrowest focus.

It is worth repeating that because the NPX provides real-time transparency into deliverables, dependencies, and ownership, SteerCo meetings are rarely used for status reporting. Colleagues at every level can access what they need directly in the NPX; SteerCos exists only to unblock issues that cannot be resolved elsewhere.

Functional Interactions

CRISP™ is not meant to replace **all** cross-functional interactions needed between Functions and Entities. It does not directly help with discussions about strategy, for instance.

Here are two examples of CF/CE interactions that happen in most initiatives:

1. During due diligence, discrepancies are found between purchase terms and financial representations. There are a number of reasons why this may legitimately happen and necessitate discussions to understand the underlying cause. Side-deals and lack of documentation rigor often surface as reasons. CRISP™'s only involvement are the NPs that represents delivery of the terms and financial documents.

2. In a carve-out scenario, the Buyer's IT SMEs decide to duplicate the Seller's ERP system rather than stand-up an entirely new platform. They map out a strategy to accomplish this objective and vet the plan with the Seller's IT SMEs. Here, after architectural and resource availability are hammered out, new CRISP™ NPs are created to reflect previously unknown deliverables.

However, it *is* meant to replace fragmented deliverable tracking and interrupt-driven ad hoc communication requests for information that can be identified, produced, and shared in advance, or as is often the case, identified in real-time.

If you find yourself in a hastily called meeting or receiving an urgent email asking for information that was known to be needed but not expressed, an NP should have been added to the NPX so it could have been addressed earlier. Likewise, if you are the one calling the meeting or sending the email, as a Consumer, you should have requested that data as part of the review process.

Transition Services Agreement Administration

The Transition Services Agreement, or TSA, defines the operational bridge that keeps the acquired or divested business running during the period between close and full separation. It formalizes what the Buyer continues to rely on from the Seller, under what conditions, and for how long. Administration of this agreement is one of the Initiative Administrator's most visible responsibilities. It ensures that every service described in the TSA—financial reporting, payroll processing, IT access, HR support, and others—remains available, controlled, and properly billed until its designated end date.

TSA administration is not limited to legal oversight. It combines operational monitoring, communication management, and record control. Workstream Leads and the Integration Management Office play supporting roles, while the Initiative Administrators coordinate across both entities to ensure each TSA item operates as intended. The process protects business continuity, prevents disputes, and provides a single source of truth for services, costs, and changes.

Purpose and Scope

The purpose of TSA administration is to maintain seamless delivery of transition services while ensuring clarity of ownership, financial transparency, and timely completion. Every Schedule A (Seller) and B (Buyer) item within the TSA minimally lists the specific service, frequency, cost, and responsible parties. Administration involves tracking these items, resolving issues through Business As Usual (BAU) requests, processing formal Change Requests (CR) when scope or duration must shift, and managing any financial adjustments that accompany each decision.

Effective administration also reinforces confidentiality, data protection, and adherence to the contract's warranty provisions. Each TSA record must remain consistent with the executed agreement, and all communications regarding it must be documented.

Business As Usual Requests

Business As Usual (BAU) requests support the day-to-day execution of the TSA. These are operational needs that fall within the agreed scope/routine activities, such as resetting credentials, updating access permissions, or generating standard reports.

Each TSA item includes one or more triggers that define when and how the service is performed. Some are *scheduled*, such as a monthly financial close; others are *event-based*, like onboarding a new hire; and some are *manual*, where either party requests assistance through the Seller's support organization.

BAU activity never alters the TSA's financial or contractual structure. It keeps services running according to plan, and every request is logged and tracked for accountability and reporting.

TSA Change Administration

When a service must be modified—expanded, reduced, or terminated—the TSA Change process applies. A Change Request is a formal modification to the agreement or its schedules, always documented in writing. The Initiative Administrators for Buyer and Seller initiate the process together, ensuring both sides have visibility and authority.

Five categories of change exist within TSA administration:

- Termination
- Reduction
- Increase
- Addition
- Term Change

Once a request is received, the Initiative Administrator determines whether a cost estimate is required. If the impact is material, an estimate is developed and scheduled for review by the relevant Steering Committee.

The committee's approval serves as the control point for any significant financial or operational alteration.

Approved changes are documented by amending the TSA schedule, including, if needed, adding a new item and reference ID that ties it to the originating service. For example, for Schedule A item "A-IT10," which covers email management, a change to begin the IT handover would be identified with a new NPX entry as "A-IT10a". Any fee adjustments are then applied to the billing cycle, and both parties receive an updated record. This process ensures that each modification remains traceable, reviewed, and properly implemented.

Exhibit A: Sample Change Request Form

The following is a listing of the fields and values from an actual change form:

- **TSA Reference.** AFIN03 – Financial Reporting GL Support
- **Request Type.** Reduction – Scope
- **Workstream.** Finance & Accounting
- **SubWorkstream.** Financial Reporting – GL Support
- **Description.** Buyer and Seller agree to reduce the service related to this item to eight hours per month, effective next billing cycle.
- **Primary Contacts.** Charlie Ferguson (Buyer), Macy Morgan (Seller)
- **Monthly Labor Cost.** $720
- **Monthly IT/Non-Labor Cost.** $0
- **Monthly Third-Party Costs.** $0
- **Total Monthly Costs.** $720

- **Methodology/Notes.** Eight hours per month at $90 per hour. Seller validated a reduction from $10,392 per month to $720 per month. Recorded in Finance & Accounting Tactical Leadership Session on July 25, 2022.

https://crispmethod.com/jmo-change-request/?cm_id=omae

Knowledge Transfer Under the TSA

Certain services are provided through the TSA, including Knowledge Transfer obligations. These are addressed in detail in the Key Artifact chapter subsection named Knowledge Transfer and should be referenced there for execution guidelines. All recorded sessions and documents related to TSA items must include their Schedule A or B reference numbers to maintain traceability.

Separation Work and Reference ID Management

As transition activities progress, specific TSA items may need temporary derivatives to support wind-down or incremental services. These additional tracking items inherit the parent reference number with a suffix to identify their relationship, such as "AIT10a" or "BLEG1d." The use of a consistent labeling structure ensures that every effort, estimate, and invoice remains linked to its origin.

Governance and Communication

The Initiative Administrators are the single point of coordination for TSA execution between the Parties. All correspondence, whether BAU or Change, must be documented in writing and archived. Steering Committee participation is reserved for material adjustments in cost, scope, or duration. The IMO supports this by maintaining repository access and ensuring that both Buyer and Seller Workstreams always operate from the latest TSA versions.

Recordkeeping and Closure

Each TSA document—schedules, amendments, and correspondence—is filed in the TSA repository. The repository is typically a section of collaboration space controlled by an IMO. Upon completion of a service, the Initiative Administrator confirms closure with both entities, validates final billing, and authorizes archival. These records serve as the definitive audit trail for the transition period.

Notes on Transition Service Agreement Documents

For post-close efficiency and effectiveness, CRISP™ recommends that the design of documents, especially a detailed TSA schedule of services, be in an easily modified and referenceable format rather than a snapshot of a spreadsheet. The reason is straightforward: The less reformatting or translation/transforming work that needs to be done to convert a legal-only document into something operational useful—cutting and pasting from a text document into a spreadsheet, for instance—the faster and more accurately the IMO TSA working artifact can be created.

Further, the TSA serves as an item-level representation of what each party in the deal needs to do and typically includes estimated delivery or end dates and financial billing information. As each item is completed (however that happens), resulting in curtailment or reductions of service that is no longer needed or adjusted for declining use, the TSA needs to be updated. Since the TSA becomes the post-close drumbeat for the initiative and typically undergoes multiple routine changes over the course of the transition, ensuring its structure and indexing scheme efficiently support item-by-item change documentation is a must-meet goal.

Last, any terms that will affect the execution of the transaction need to be easily extracted from where they reside in the main agreement for use as Initiative reference documents. This would include terms related to cross-entity billing, timing constraints, etc. If handled as an addendum or standalone (formatting-wise) section with deal-sensitive information located elsewhere, legal can simply provide the entire section(s) to the IMO without having to create a redacted or edited version of the entire agreement or pages.

Summary

Transition Services Agreement Administration is the backbone of operational stability following a transaction. It balances the need for ongoing support with the discipline of formal documentation, ensuring that every service delivered under the TSA is accounted for, governed, and ultimately concluded without ambiguity. By managing both Business As Usual and Change activity under a single administrative structure, the initiative preserves continuity, transparency, and trust between Buyer and Seller.

Knowledge Transfer

There is a wide spectrum of situations in which knowledge transfer from the Seller to the Buyer is necessary. Not every initiative requires it, but when it does, the consequences of doing it poorly are immediate and costly.

Having established how CRISP™ defines execution accountability and deliverable ownership, this area of focus involves deliberately transferring operational knowledge using those concepts.

Effective Knowledge Transfer (KT) ensures that the Buyer's teams can assume responsibility for processes, systems, and deliverables with full continuity, while the Seller exits cleanly, with minimum effort and, ideally, zero unplanned post-initiative activity. Within the CRISP™ framework, KT is not an ad hoc free-for-all; it is a governed process grounded in precision, traceability, and single-session efficiency.

Purpose and Context

Knowledge Transfer bridges the final stage of execution between entities. It enables the Buyer to sustain operations once transitional dependencies on the Seller have ended. The purpose is twofold:

- To preserve institutional understanding that cannot be captured through artifacts alone.
- To create a permanent, accessible record of that understanding within the Knowledge Transfer Repository (KTR).

Whereas artifacts such as the Request List and NPX define what needs to be exchanged, KT defines how expertise is transferred and validated. It exists to prevent repetition, ambiguity, and unnecessary reliance on individuals once the Seller's obligations conclude.

Core Principles

KT under CRISP™ follows a small set of strict principles:

- **Buyer-Initiated.** The Buyer must submit all KT requests in writing through an established artifact, typically the Request List or equivalent structured request tool. Chat messages or informal discussions **never** constitute a valid KT request.
- **Seller-Owned.** The Seller owns and delivers the session. The obligation includes preparing materials, ensuring content accuracy, and recording the session.
- **Single-Session Discipline.** The objective is to deliver one comprehensive session per topic. Repeated or piecemeal training indicates poor preparation or incomplete scoping.
- **Recorded and Indexed.** Every session is recorded, named, and stored within the KTR using consistent file conventions that trace back to the governing deliverable (usually the TSA) or schedule item.
- **Transparent Oversight.** The Initiative Administrator ensures adherence to process, confirms proper documentation, and verifies repository integrity.

Preparation and Setup

Every KT engagement begins with understanding the Buyer's intent. The Initiative Administrator facilitates the initial request review to confirm purpose and feasibility:

1. **Define the Intent.** Determine whether the Buyer seeks to assume ownership of a process immediately or at a future transition point.
2. **Confirm Prerequisites.** Verify that Buyer participants have completed prerequisite training or possess required baseline access.
3. **Assess Risk.** Identify whether information-security or operational risks exist that would limit knowledge sharing. If elevated privileges

are necessary but restricted, the Seller should proceed with KT while clearly documenting the access limitation.

4. **Negotiate Scope and Timing.** Establish the specific topics to be covered, the responsible Seller experts, and the schedule. The Initiative Administrator reviews these parameters to confirm that they align with the initiative's transition plan.

Once the scope is agreed, both parties understand that the Seller will deliver a single, recorded session meeting the above conditions.

Execution and Recording

A CRISP™-aligned KT session is structured, not conversational. The Seller begins with a short preamble acknowledging that the contents are subject to the confidentiality and data-handling provisions of the governing agreement. The video should open with a clear "slate" listing:

- Deliverable or process name
- Seller presenter(s) and Buyer participants
- Session topic and date

The Seller reads the slate aloud to establish an audible record before proceeding.

Once recording begins, the focus is on clarity and completeness: demonstrating the process, explaining decisions, and identifying any variations that may exist during transition. Participants are encouraged to ask questions and press for clarity.

Upon completion, the Seller posts the recording and supporting documentation to the designated KTR location. The Initiative Administrator validates the upload, ensures file traceability, and confirms that naming conventions are correctly applied. A typical convention links each file to its controlling deliverable or reference number. For example, "FIN-04_Payroll-KT-20250312" is related to the TSA item FIN-04 that deals with Payroll.

Governance and Compliance

While the KT process is operational and interactive, its governance is contractual. Every recorded session constitutes part of the formal record of transfer. Each is therefore subject to any applicable confidentiality, warranty, and intellectual-property provisions.

The Initiative Administrator serves as both arbiter and steward:

- Arbiter, to ensure Buyer requests are legitimate, necessary, and properly scoped.
- Steward, to guarantee the resulting content is securely stored, consistently cataloged, and accessible to those who require it for continuity.

In CRISP™, KT sessions are not ad hoc trainings; they are deliverables governed by the same precision and accountability that apply to any artifact. Each entry in the KTR is discoverable, linked through the NPX, and traceable to its request origin.

Integration with CRISP™ Artifacts

Knowledge Transfer does not stand apart from other CRISP™ components; it interacts dynamically with them:

- **Request List.** Formal KT requests originate here, providing transparency to both Buyer and Seller workstreams.
- **NPX.** KT sessions often resolve open intersections between deliverables by codifying tacit knowledge into explicit, reusable content.
- **Colleague Roster.** Identifies who delivered and who received each session, preserving accountability and lineage.
- **Knowledge Transfer Repository.** Serves as the single authoritative source for all recorded KT sessions, slides, and supporting materials.

Together, these artifacts create a complete communication and traceability loop. When used correctly, no element of transferred knowledge exists outside the system of record.

Benefits and Outcomes

When executed with discipline, Knowledge Transfer achieves several outcomes fundamental to CRISP™:

- **Continuity without Dependence.** The Buyer can operate critical processes without Seller intervention.
- **Reduced Redundancy**. Single-session recording eliminates repeated trainings and inconsistent messaging.
- **Traceable Accountability**. Each KT instance has a clear owner, date, and link to governing deliverables.
- **Operational Readiness for AI and Automation**. Recorded, structured knowledge becomes analyzable input for future process optimization tools.

Closing Reflection

Knowledge Transfer within CRISP™ transforms a traditionally informal exchange into a measurable deliverable. It broadens the scope from teaching to documenting and converts memory into evidence. The Initiative Administrator ensures that each session reinforces precision and preserves operational knowledge long after human involvement ends. The result is lasting clarity: knowledge that remains accessible, auditable, and ready to power whatever comes next in the initiative's evolution.

NOTES

IMPLEMENTATION

So, you've decided CRISP™ makes sense in your situation—now what? This chapter will walk through the activities needed to successfully adopt CRISP™ in your environment.

With the exception of Key Artifact creation, 80% of the effort is spent on communication. Specifically, initiating intentional messaging between appropriate parties. CRISP™ provides a supporting end-to-end messaging plan, complete with sample language and automation opportunities.

Also, keep in mind that CRISP™ was designed to leverage an organization's existing technology. Rather than re-inventing or introducing new technologies, CRISP™ leverages what Parties already have in place. For core functionality that is missing, simple, low-cost, generic point solutions can often be substituted with little additional expense or specialized training.

Pre-Adoption Activities

A number of critical activities are needed before attempting to adopt CRISP™. The first is the understanding and acceptance of the assumptions on which the model depends (see the Assumptions section in the Foundation Chapter). Then, depending on the situation, all or some of the following may be required:

1) C-suite or partner buy-in and approval
2) Cross-functional senior-level buy-in
3) Cross-entity senior-level buy-in
4) Funding approval
5) Personnel/advisor assignments or hires

Once the alignment of the senior-level Colleagues has been established, the actual adoption for the remaining contributors can take place. This ensures that support from the top can be relied on should friction regarding change occur deeper in an organization (or with external suppliers).

Existing IMOs

To be clear, CRISP™ adoption by an IMO is not an all-or-nothing proposition across all initiatives. It can be, but it doesn't have to be.

Not surprisingly, the recommendation is to pilot CRISP™ with a full end-to-end adoption. Full end-to-end means the entire process, starting with the inception of the initiative. In CRISP™ lingo, the Preparation Phase. Senior executives acting as Colleagues come under the same method as rank-and-file integration participants, including their roles as Producers and Consumers of Nexus Point Content. This will provide excellent feedback for all facets of an initiative and where potential issues may arise.

Alternatively, introducing CRISP™ in a peri-close fashion (with sufficient time to introduce and socialize CRISP™ pre-close) can also work, although the inferred message delivered by senior execs using CRISP™ early on should not be underestimated.

New IMOs

Starting up a new IMO is the ideal time to adopt CRISP™. Using CRISP™'s protocols as a ready-reference framework, IMOs can quickly establish alignment across the enterprise and trusted suppliers. With little institutional inertia to overcome, the new organization has a unique opportunity to build its culture and operating rhythm around clarity, transparency, and disciplined communication, values that CRISP™ formalizes through its standardized artifacts and information flows.

The first weeks of a new IMO's existence often coincide with a honeymoon period, when change is expected and enthusiasm is high. Leaders can use this moment to introduce CRISP™ not as a tool, but as the foundation for how the IMO functions. Establishing document governance, defining the Colleague Roster, and setting up the NPX during this window positions the team to scale without the confusion that often follows rapid onboarding. Once the pace accelerates, it becomes far harder to insert structure into established behaviors.

For a new IMO, the benefits of adopting CRISP™ early include:

1. **Accelerated onboarding.** Roles, responsibilities, and access points are clearly defined from day one.
2. **Immediate operational credibility.** Consistent terminology and structured workflows reassure both Buyer and Seller teams that decisions are being tracked and executed.
3. **Reduced friction.** Centralized artifacts eliminate redundant requests and misaligned communications.
4. **Predictable governance.** Each decision or escalation follows a defined path, minimizing confusion when pressure mounts.
5. **Sustained efficiency.** As new initiatives are started or existing ones evolve, the same framework scales seamlessly across functions and entities.

The difference between a reactive IMO and a disciplined one often traces back to its first month. By anchoring early behaviors in CRISP™ principles, leadership signals a commitment to precision and mutual accountability. Those signals shape how Colleagues communicate, how decisions are made, and ultimately, how effectively the integration or separation performs. The best time to adopt CRISP™ is before patterns harden, when the organization is still defining what "normal" looks like.

No IMO

CRISP™ can also be deployed where no IMO exists. The CRISP™ Tactical Field Guides (TFGs) are designed to be executed without specialized organizational support beyond the steering committee(s). The architecture is designed to be self-defining and self-maintaining, reducing administrative costs connected with the initiative.

Deployment in this environment works best with an executive champion providing political support to an Initiative Administrator who facilitates SteerCo and WL meetings, monitors key Artifacts, and follows and enforces TFG protocols. See the resourcing roles section for tips on who performs best in this scenario.

Colleague/Stakeholder Initial Level-Setting

Alignment by setting expectations is the first order of business when approaching a CRISP™ deployment. The CRISP™ Presentations TFG has messaging tailored to each Colleague group, highlighting the specific benefits each group will enjoy by using the method. Messaging also includes the obligations of the primary roles (Consumer and Producer), overviews of key event timing, and appropriate reviews of the core set of CRISP™ artifacts. On-boarding using the recommended presentations is designed to take less than an hour, per group.

In addition to explaining the mechanics of CRISP™, this initial level setting also actively seeks to surface resistance to the method so that steps can be taken early to address potential trouble spots as the initiative unfolds.

Role of Service Desk(s)

A well-functioning Service Desk (SD) is essential not only for implementing CRISP™ but also for making the transition as smooth and frictionless as possible. Proper SD alignment and definition leverage people who are already in place, while at the same time potentially reducing some of the administrative burden on the IMO. This applies to service desks of all Parties involved in the Initiative.

Early in the implementation process, clarity around what is expected of the SD relative to CRISP™, as well as an unambiguous understanding of what the SD will be providing, before, during, and after the transition. This is an oft-neglected activity that, if left to the last minute or ignored entirely, can introduce immense noise, nail-biting, and chaos into what should and can be a quiet and orderly process.

Depending on the size and scope of existing SDs, the range of service and support can vary dramatically. In a best-case scenario, the SD can handle all support required for on boarding and off boarding employees, plus network access, field application/hardware, and process support questions that transitioning Stakeholders will have surrounding the Initiative.

Where "one-stop shopping" is not available and support is distributed across functional areas, consideration should be given to creating a temporary structure as part of the SD specifically to triage all Initiative support requests and then route them to the appropriate group.

In situations where the SD is weak (limited scope and depth of service offered) or non-existent, special attention should be given to how inevitable questions will be handled and support activities will be performed.

3rd-Party Players

While 3rd-party players (external technical SMEs, advisors, consultants, etc.) can technically be defined as stakeholders, their introduction to CRISP™ and their commitment to following the method require a different treatment than rank-and-file Colleagues. The primary reason is that there is an additional contractual element that can be used to the contracting Party's advantage to ensure compliance throughout the initiative.

Of course, the recommendation is to include terms in 3rd-Party-engagement agreements that explicitly specify CRISP™ as the cross-entity information management method. Starting at this point with any 3rd Party provides an automatic backstop, should compliance become an issue.

Technology Platform Prep

Technology Platform Preparation

CRISP™ is intentionally technology agnostic. Execution does not depend on any proprietary platform, software brand, or integrated system. Instead, CRISP™ relies on a small set of baseline technology capabilities that most organizations already possess, or can provision quickly, without introducing new operational burden.

Minimum Technology Capabilities

At an operational level, CRISP™ requires only the following foundational capabilities:

- Reliable email and phone access for all Colleagues
- Access controlled shared storage capable of hosting common master files such as the NPX and Colleague Roster, or functional equivalents
- A spreadsheet or BI capable application that supports column level filtering, or an equivalent proxy
- Real time collaboration tools that support live sessions and recording for working discussions

These days, the ubiquity of these technologies are well established and should be leveraged.

Why IM/DM tools create unnecessary risk

Instant or direct messaging tools are neither required nor recommended for routine execution. Their use should be limited to unanticipated or emergency situations. Ad hoc outreach for information that was known in advance disrupts execution, introduces unnecessary noise, and frequently results in data exchanges that bypass the NPX. When this occurs, information gaps are created, additional rework is introduced, and Producers can become disconnected from delivery commitments and ownership expectations.

Adapting Existing Platforms

Organizations enter initiatives with varying degrees of technical and organizational debt. For this reason, a CRISP™ compliant evaluation tool is available to licensees to assist with implementation . The purpose of this AI assisted tool is to assess the suitability of existing platforms against CRISP™ execution requirements, not to mandate replacement.

After results are pressure tested against the usage goals, a tool by tool configuration guide is produced. This guide specifies exactly what must be enabled, structured, configured, or constrained within the current application set to support optimized execution behavior during the initiative.

Subsequent sections of this chapter address how previously defined protocols can be adapted to fit the realities of a specific environment.

Confidentiality and Security

Confidentiality is a high priority requirement throughout the full arc of an M&A initiative, with heightened sensitivity during early phases. CRISP™ does not prescribe a specific document management system, but any platform used should minimally support the capabilities outlined below.

Segregation and Permission Control

Document management or collaboration tools should allow:

- Easy segregation of documents and permissions without IT intervention
- Folder structures aligned to defined Workstreams, with the ability for Workstreams to create sub-structures dynamically
- Access control monitored through the Colleague Roster

This structure supports execution flexibility while maintaining clear ownership and accountability.

External Access

Platforms must support controlled access from outside the host organization's environment. For example:

- During due diligence, a seller may provide discovery documents in a secure location accessible to a limited set of buyer-side Colleagues
- Access is granted on a need-to-know basis and adjusted as conditions change

Internal, External, Public, and Private Channels

During an initiative, information flows across multiple entities and parties. In this context:

- **Public** means accessible to all Colleagues across entities
- **Private** means restricted to a defined subset of individuals
- **Internal** and **external** are relative to entity boundaries

Examples include:

- Seller contracts shared privately and externally for buyer due diligence
- Employee transition lists that begin as internal and private, then become external at close
- Post-close suppliers requiring limited access to seller data that remains private even after the initiative concludes

Platforms must support these distinctions without forcing duplicative repositories or manual workarounds.

Restricted File Access and Maintenance

CRISP™ strongly recommends that all initiative-related materials reside in a single, logically structured central repository. While not all documents should be broadly accessible, all should be locatable within that structure.

Responsibility for protecting confidential or sensitive information rests with the Producer. This can be implemented in two primary ways:

File-Level Controls

Highly sensitive documents may be stored in the shared repository with access restricted to specific individuals. The Producer maintains responsibility for granting, reviewing, and adjusting permissions.

Group or Channel-Based Controls

During due diligence, large sets of sensitive documents are often shared with a small, defined audience that may include external advisors. In these cases:

- Channel- or area-based access is more efficient than locking files individually
- Metadata indexes may be used to track review status, reviewer identity, timing, and findings

- Existing platforms often support this capability, or can be configured to do so with minimal effort

Use of the Colleague Roster to track special access privileges is recommended.

An alternative approach is entity-level segmentation, where each entity maintains its own controlled area within the repository and manages access independently on a need-to-know basis.

AI-assisted adoption

Because of the variety and depth of technical and organizational debt, a CRISP™-compliant AI-powered configuration service is available for implementation. The service determines the fit (or not) given the properties of the active platforms. After pressure-testing the results, an app-by-app configuration guide is produced, ensuring that what is needed for optimizing the specific initiative execution is included in the available technology.

Key Suppliers

It's rare for Initiatives to be executed without needing outside help. Whether it's help with strategy, due diligence, execution management, or technical assistance, any and all external resources who have access to the Initiative documents and people need to be accounted for in the Colleague Roster and introduced to how CRISP™ works and the Protocols in force.

Resistance Is to Be Expected

Initial resistance to CRISP™ from suppliers is common. It lasts until they experience the benefit, which comes very quickly. The most obvious benefit is smoother, quicker, and higher-quality access to the information they need to service their patch of the initiative. Here are some of the arguments you are likely to encounter, along with the corresponding counter-arguments:

1. **Creates extra work.** How? Producers are responsible for delivering their NPC (Nexus Point Content), regardless of who they work for. Since the only administrative work is placing the output in the NPX repository and marking the NP with the completion date, the "extra" work for the Producer is less than 30 seconds. For the Consumer, it's even less work. The only thing they have to do is express interest in the data they need, flagging those NPs with their identifier, and aligning with the Producer on date and format. And if the deliverable is a single piece of data, like a yes or no decision or an internal account code, it's even faster because the NPX is the actual source of truth; no other inquiry is necessary. CRISP™ also has an aspirational goal of putting Consumers no more than three clicks away from what they need.
2. **We're using our own management tools.** Great! So are we. If there is cross-functional/cross-entity information that needs to be exchanged, the NPX is the tool that handles it (with close to zero administrative overhead). Everyone benefits.

3. **Our people aren't trained to use it.** CRISP™ requires no specialized training, beyond the use of email, spreadsheets, and a portal or repository tool like Teams or SharePoint. A 30-minute introduction with ongoing ad hoc support is all that's needed for Producers and Consumers to be on-boarded and up to speed. The same is true for external functional/technical SMEs. Follow the simply-defined CRISP™ protocols and everything else falls into place.

Low Compliance Equals Loss of Efficiency

External consultants, advisors, technicians, or administrative help are naturally part of any Initiative's ecosystem. They need information and data available in the collaboration platform, NPX, and other CRISP™ key artifacts. Just like any other Colleague, their contact and access information gets added to the Roster. If they are using the NPX, they should tag the NPs they are interested in just like any other Consumer would.

Changes are inevitable during any Transaction. CRISP™'s design is efficient in communicating changes. As has been mentioned, the most granular protocol around change says that Producers are responsible for communicating any changes to the NP (delays, formatting, etc.) to Consumers of the NP as soon as they are known.

So, if compliance is low (externals, as Consumers, are not indicating that they need anything) and changes to the NPs occur (and they do), the Producers will have no way of contacting them other than through added effort. If that effort is unsuccessful or not performed, unnecessary gaps in communication that could have been avoided may occur. This can also lead to uncontrolled inquiries for routine information, causing further disruption and potential delay.

Ideally, compliance should be voluntary, but service agreements can be easily crafted to include rewards for compliance or penalties for noncompliance with CRISP™ protocols. This should be vetted as part of the supplier engagement negotiations.

Management Consulting Firms and CRISP™

Management consulting firms bring their own methods and protocols to assist clients during a Transaction. These approaches are valuable; however, unless CRISP™ has already been licensed and incorporated into their practice, those methods will not perfectly align with CRISP™. This is expected and entirely acceptable.

Because every Transaction involves at least two Parties, CRISP™ is designed to serve as the common connector across all. Each Party is free to manage its internal processes as it chooses. The key, however, lies in eliminating duplication of effort, reducing noise, and ensuring the efficiency gains that CRISP™ enables.

To achieve these benefits, there must be a joint agreement that all cross-functional and cross-entity information exchanges will be handled through CRISP™ and its Key Artifacts. This applies to all management groups, whether they operate as an Integration Management Office (IMO), Project Management Office (PMO), or external consultants responsible for sequencing and resource allocation.

Nexus Points exist independent of who manages the initiative. Producers of those Nexus Points remain responsible for delivering the required content, while Workstream Leads are accountable for ensuring their Producers and Consumers comply. Registration of Colleagues, both internal and external, is intentionally streamlined. This ensures contributors have access to the information they need and that obligations to external Consumers and Producers are clearly identified.

So, if one Party or its advisors employs a proprietary method to manage internal Workstreams, that is not an obstacle. As long as cross-functional and cross-entity exchanges are executed in alignment with CRISP™ Protocols and Artifacts adopted by the counterpart Party, the benefits of clarity, speed, and cost reduction remain intact.

For consulting and advisory firms interested in extending these advantages to their clients, CRISP™ provides consultant and advisory licensing options.

Transition

Post-LOI Initiative Hints

CRISP™ re-centers initiative execution on Producer-responsible deliverables, most of which are known well in advance of the transaction close. This section outlines how CRISP™ manages transition-related activity both leading up to and following the close date.

Pre-Close Agreement

To ensure a smooth, issue-free transition, CRISP™ recommends resolving as many non-controversial items as possible prior to close. Administrative activities are the most straightforward, including, if needed, identifying and configuring document-sharing and workflow platforms to ensure momentum on Day 1.

The specifics of which Key Artifacts are required will vary depending on the transaction type, complexity, and known transition risks. CRISP™ does not dictate these but enables their early identification so Producers can begin preparing well before close.

Transaction-Related Billing

Transaction-related billing covers those TSA elements requiring billing and payment outside the core financial terms of the transaction. CRISP™ recommends two distinct categories, each with its own invoice:

1. **Fixed-rate service billing.** Recurring charges for predefined services, typically tied to stable resources or systems. This should represent the bulk of TSA items.
2. **Variable-rate service billing.** Usage-based or time-based charges, such as SME access or system utilization. This allows for ad hoc billing events related to unforeseen changes or findings.

Line-item detail must be organized by TSA Item and reflect any active Change Requests. Updated billing terms should be noted only if they differ from prior invoices, in which case the CR reference must be included.

Pre- and Post-Transaction Change Management

Change management during a transaction, whether before or after close, generally falls into three categories:

1. **Timing-related.** Milestone or deadline adjustments.
2. **Service-related.** TSA additions, reductions, or re-scoping.
3. **SME-related.** Impacts on SME involvement due to resource changes or conflicts.

All changes must follow formal protocols. CRISP™ requires that all changes be reflected in TSA Change Forms, Request List, or NPX, with confirmation from Buyer and Seller Workstream Leads. Informal requests are not recognized and carry no escalation support if problematic or unfulfilled. All parties should agree to Change Management protocols, ideally prior to the legal close.

SCALING CRISP™

There are two ways CRISP™ can be scaled:

1. By the initiative, expanding or contracting one transaction at a time.
2. By the enterprise, where initiatives of various types are executing simultaneously over time.

This section describes single initiatives; enterprise scaling is outside the scope of this book. If you are faced with running parallel initiatives, contact me for a private session to discuss the ramifications and how easily CRISP™ supports this type of use. But first …

Understanding how to scale CRISP™ begins with acknowledging its most important design attribute: every cross-functional/cross-entity (CF/CE) data exchange is anchored at the individual level. Communication moves between specific Producers and specific Consumers, not between teams, departments, or systems. This foundation gives CRISP™ a structural advantage when initiatives grow in size or complexity. Scaling does not require new layers of coordination or additional workflow constructs; it only requires continued adherence to clear, synchronized communication behaviors.

Since CRISP™ is tech- and business-segment agnostic, its Key Artifacts can be rendered in any existing ecosystem and, as such, it behaves consistently across different organizational types, entity structures, and industry contexts. These properties give it a neutral footprint that remains stable regardless of initiative size or scope.

Why CRISP™ Scales

CRISP™ scales because the core mechanics do not change when initiatives expand (or are large to begin with). Ownership, purpose, and timing remain clear. Producers and Consumers stay aligned because the constructs that guide them do not rely on organizational adjacency. Messaging behaviors are agreed to, and they preserve the signal as new contributors enter the initiative.

Nothing in CRISP™ requires reconfiguration, recursion, or structural recomposition as the initiative grows. The same fields, the same communication rules, and the same clarity mechanisms support a higher volume of detail without introducing noise or delay.

Of course, scaling anything is not a monolithic or 1-dimensional exercise. What follows are descriptions covering the most common single-initiative dimensions. You'll find much of it will feel repetitive, and that's a good thing.

Scaling Across Initiative Size and Complexity

CRISP™ is optimized for mid-sized and large initiatives where the volume of CF/CE communication can start out big or increase rapidly. As contributor counts, Workstream interactions, and entity relationships grow or change, the communication model remains consistent. Coordination does not collapse into ad hoc meetings or a proliferation of trackers because deliverables remain anchored to individual Producers and individual Consumers, no matter how many there are.

Note: Mid-market companies stand to benefit significantly from this model. Limited execution resources amplify the consequences of misalignment. CRISP™ reduces wasted effort by ensuring contributors share a consistent understanding of ownership, purpose, and timing, even when capacity is tight.

Scaling Across Technology Environments

CRISP™ can be rendered with a company's existing tools. Because no proprietary system is required, organizations avoid the scaling bottlenecks, disconnects, and delays commonly associated with new software adoption. As the number of contributors increases, the artifacts continue to function cleanly. Layouts, naming conventions, and fields do not change. This stability prevents the drift that often occurs when multiple platforms are used concurrently.

Technology independence also accelerates the onboarding of new contributors. They enter an artifact environment that matches tools they already know, reducing training and avoiding delays caused by unfamiliar interfaces.

Scaling Across Business Segments

CRISP™ supports Buyers, Sellers, Advisors, and other partners in any segment. It behaves consistently whether the organization operates in the private mid-market space or in a large public enterprise environment. The communication-centric structure does not require customization to accommodate industry specifics or organizational models. It simply clarifies who needs what, from whom, and by when.

Note: Mid-market companies benefit from this universality. They can operate with the same communication clarity used by larger organizations without increasing their operating overhead.

Scaling Through the Key Artifacts

The Key Artifacts absorb scale without modification. Each artifact maintains the same structure regardless of the number of contributors or deliverables. Ownership fields remain explicit. Timing fields remain visible. Relationships between Producers and Consumers remain clear. As volume increases, the artifacts do not become more complex; they simply contain more entries. This avoids the need for alternative tracking tools and eliminates the common drift toward decentralized spreadsheets and multiple sources of truth.

Scaling Through Run Mode Discipline

Run Mode behaviors act as stabilizers. Tactical Field Guides and messaging protocols define how contributors communicate. When initiatives scale, these behaviors ensure that timing agreements are respected, updates are meaningful, and ownership is clear. The result is predictable information flow, even in high-pressure environments. Plus, the reduction of non-value-add time that results from following CRISP™ allows more time to focus on higher-value execution activities and issues.

Organizational Conditions That Support Scaling

CRISP™ requires contributors to maintain straightforward, disciplined communication habits. Timely responses, clear ownership, and adherence to delivery agreements (timing and quality) are the minimum conditions for scale. When these behaviors are present, CRISP™ maintains its signal as the initiative size grows. When they are absent, any initiative struggles, regardless of the toolset being used.

Common Scaling Failure Patterns

CRISP™ prevents several typical failure patterns that emerge as initiatives expand:

- Adding additional status and approval loops, which retards progress.
- Relying on unrestrained, tool-driven workflows, creating unnecessary noise.
- Implementing well-intentioned but excessive dependency tracking, introducing confusion and more work instead of clarity.

CRISP™ avoids these patterns by keeping communication anchored at the individual level and by embedding dependencies within NP-negotiated timing and delivery agreements rather than in external maps.

Scaling Summary

CRISP™ scales because it is built on reproducible individual communication behaviors. These behaviors remain stable at any initiative size. Its tech- and business-segment agnostic design ensures that scaling feels familiar and does not introduce friction or new, complicated things to learn. And its structural clarity delivers outsized benefits to all Parties, but especially those companies operating with limited execution capacity.

NOTES

CLOSE

CRISP™ represents a transformative departure from traditional project/program management practices. It is designed to address the unique needs of M&A deals and mitigate the noise and confusion that often accompany these initiatives.

By focusing on communications between Colleagues, CRISP™ optimizes vetting, accessing, and updating mission-critical information, eliminating the need to hold duplicative and wasteful SME-driven requirement gathering sessions, repetitive and non-actionable status sessions, or spend time chasing missing deliverables. Fewer non-productive meetings = less stress for all involved.

Further, the approach leverages the specific knowledge Colleagues have about their personal workloads relative to what the initiative needs them to do, eliminating previous time and effort invested in discovering, documenting, and maintaining CF/CE dependency relationships.

Finally, because CRISP™ is tech-agnostic, using existing, basic work tools, no technical debt is incurred during adoption, and use can commence quickly with no tool-specific investment or training required to get started.

Using CRISP™ ensures the people ultimately responsible for initiative execution success get the information they need, in the form they expect it, on or before they need it.

If designing a bespoke implementation from this book is not the objective, complete versions of the Key Artifacts and Tactical Field Guides, along with optional coaching, training, and advisory services, are available through a CRISP™ license from Exertus, Inc.; scan the QR code or visit the URL to explore licensing options.

https://crispmethod.com/faq/how-is-crisp-licensed?cm_id=omae

Appendix A: Lexicon

CRISP™ uses a number of commonly used words/terms with special definitions. Where these are used in documentation, they are capitalized, i.e., "Consumer."

CF/CE

1. Cross Functional/Cross Entity communication is the key focus of CRISP™.
2. It is where a critical majority of execution issues emanate from and is seldom directly addressed in traditional initiative management models or tools.
3. CF/CE is also the overarching constraint when it comes to identifying and recording NPX items; inter-Workstream or inter-

Entity issues are best solved/tracked within the function or entity where they occurred and not in the NPX.

Change Request (CR)

1. Changes to various parts of the initiative are to be expected from the start to the finish. CRISP™ uses a simple mechanism to start, negotiate, and finalize any change that will impact the transaction in a concise and repeatable way.
2. For example, CRISP™'s TSA CRs are 1-page forms that tersely describe the requested or necessary changes. They are indexed to the TSA item(s) that they apply to.
3. IAs jointly review, approve, negotiate, or reject CRs, prior to obtaining approvals from the relevant parties (designated owners of the affected TSA items).
4. See the chapter on Implementation for detailed recommendations on how CRs can be managed with a minimum of effort.

Colleague

1. Traditional project and program management vernacular use the term "stakeholder" to refer to any individual, group, or organization that can affect, be affected by, or perceive itself to be affected by a project or program. This list can be extensive, including customers, investors, regulatory bodies, or community groups, to name just a few. Rarely are individuals enumerated when stakeholder groups are identified, which makes direct communication difficult.
2. In contrast, CRISP™ uses the label "*Colleague*" to specifically describe a single individual who is actually doing work on the initiative and needs to interact outside of their normal Workstream or Entity associations.

3. Important: where a transaction includes the movement of people from one entity to another, in contrast with a purely financial or legal deal, the transitioning employees are not generally considered *Colleagues*; they are mainly stakeholders, as few play an active role in the actual execution of the transaction.

4. See *Colleague Roster* in *Key Artifacts*.

Consumer

1. *Consumers* create, identify, and use the *Content* in the *NPX* to fulfill their roles for the initiative.

2. *Consumers* have an obligation to monitor *NPs* and interact with *Producers* according to established *Protocols* to establish delivery dates, expected deliverable quality, and any non-standardized requests.

3. CRISP™ allows *Consumers* to also be *Producers* when needed, and vice versa.

Content

1. CRISP™ uses the word *Content* to refer to any piece of *CF/CE* data or information (documents, diagrams, pictures, audio, or video) required to be exchanged.

2. To be clear, by way of an example, even though a network engineer must know the information necessary to operate the technical components and understand the IT policies in place that bound the use of the technology, that content is not what this use of *Content* refers to. Continuing this example, a list of employees who will need new network accounts or whose accounts will need to be terminated tied to the Transaction is regarded as Content.

3. *Content* can be represented as a single item, like a tax ID number or something more complicated, like a document reflecting analysis of the cultural composition of an acquisition target. The "trick" to recognizing *Content* is to perform a simple test: If the information is exclusively used within a single *Workstream,* it is not content in the context of CRISP™. But if the information has use outside of a *Workstream* (from *CF/CE* sources), that is *Content.*
4. Using this definition and the *Key Artifacts*, a primary goal of CRISP™ is to make any *Content* available in three clicks or less for any *Colleague.*
5. See *Nexus Point, Nexus Point Content,* and *Nexus Point Exchange.*

Entity

1. In the context of CRISP™, an *Entity* is typically a legal organization under or through which a *Colleague* operates. For a divestiture, you could easily have several different entities beyond just the Buyer and Seller involved:
    a. Buyer
    b. Seller
    c. Buyer's integration SMEs
    d. Buyer's technology SMEs
    e. Buyer's HR SMEs
2. *Entities* are reflected in the *NPX* data and the initiative *Colleague Roster* and serve to identify org-level accountability and activity.
3. CRISP™ delineates between the term "*Party*" and *Entity*, which are sometimes used interchangeably.
4. See *Party*

Granularity

1. *Granularity* in the context of CRISP™ refers to how detailed the information or data that needs to be exchanged needs to be. This will vary widely as some *NPC* will be single values, like a tax ID number or a yes or no decision, or complex items delivered as documents or document sets, like asset inventories or product catalogs.
2. Care should be taken in deciding the appropriate levels of *Granularity*, as too detailed results in increased administrative work, and too general results in additional work to get clarity.

High Fidelity Observation (HFO)

1. *HFO* is the CRISP™ term to describe a level of observation that the *Producer-Deliverable-Consumer* model, as expressed through the *NPX* and other required *Key Artifacts,* provides.
2. It is high fidelity, meaning the detail available from CRISP™ allows *Granular* views not typically associated with other management methods.
3. *HFO* can be enhanced by performing a wide variety of offline analyses of the *NPX.* This is particularly valuable after CRISP™ has been used for a number of initiatives, where trends or patterns based on past behavior can be identified.

Hierarchical Filtering

1. *Hierarchical Filtering* is when upstream (in an organization's reporting structure) personnel alter, withhold, or in any way distort or retard the delivery of *Nexus Point Content* from the actual *Producer* to the *Consumer.*

2. CRISP™ acknowledges and encourages the necessity for peer or managerial review within the *Producer's Workstream* processes, but expects that activity to be done as part of a *Workstream* process, prior to the *Producer* actually delivering the *NPC*. This is where a *Workstream's* quality process should kick in. The alternative (highly discouraged) is to make the manager the *Producer*, which also transfers responsibility, which is inaccurate in this scenario. That means participating in *Producer* sessions and answering questions from *Consumers*. Since managers are not the ones doing the work, it is likely that familiarity with the content is not as deep as the author/creator's, and that any questions or alterations must be translated back to the source. This adds unnecessary messaging time and risk to the deliverable. It also creates potential escalation issues.

3. See the section on the Shannon-Weaver communication model for technical reasons why this is not a good thing, and the Governance section for issues related to *Producers'* responsibility and accountability.

Integration Management Office (IMO)

1. These are the orgs within the primary *Parties* who coordinate the activities of the initiative.

2. CRISP™ makes no distinction between when coordination activities involving an *IMO* occur relative to the arc of initiative. Whether it's end-to-end management or just post-close integration activities, CRISP™ fully supports the *IMO*.

3. Sometimes these orgs are called and function as traditional Program Management Offices (PMOs), or there can be separate units used for pre-close and post-close activity.

4. Regardless of the label, *IMOs* have the responsibility of facilitating the necessary ceremonies or collaboration sessions (including *WL* and *SteerCo*) and maintenance of the *NPX* and other key, initiative-level artifacts.
5. *IMOs* are also responsible for tracking and dispositioning *COs* and updating the *TSA* to reflect its current state.

Initiative Administrator (IA)

With CRISP™, the notion of a "manager" overseeing and guiding collective effort is replaced by an "administrator" responsible for monitoring Key Artifact compliance/veracity and facilitating Key Events.

The IA also coordinates any needed escalation action.

Knowledge Transfer Repository (KTR)

1. Depending on the contours of the deal, one or more of the *Parties* may be asked to conduct "knowledge transfer" from one *Entity* to another. Since this work is usually described in general ways in the purchase/sale agreement, the CRISP™ *KTR* serves as the record that knowledge transfer was performed.
2. The *KTR* can be configured to store whatever documentation or media is appropriate for the *Parties* and should be available in view-only access for *Colleagues* who are registered in the CRISP™ *Colleague Roster Key Artifact.*
3. *NPs* should be created to indicate who the *Producer* is that will be delivering knowledge transfer (KT).
4. See *Change Requests (CR)*; *TSA* and *Colleague Roster* in *Key Artifacts.*

Milestone

1. *Milestones* are date (and sometimes time) markers to serve as alignment mechanisms as the initiative progresses. CRISP™ has a number of embedded Milestones tied to specific phases and events.
2. The *Model* allows any number of *Milestones* to be defined through a facilitated cross-functional process, but the fewer *Milestones,* the better, as each *Milestone* usually requires a stop in forward progress.
3. See *Milestone Schedule* in *Key Artifact.*

Model

1. The term *Model* is used to describe the various specific designs (data and process) that comprise CRISP™.
2. Generally, when the word *Model* is used, it means that the component being discussed has been specifically designed for modification.

Nexus Point Exchange (NPX)

1. The *Nexus Point Exchange* is the repository for all *NPs*. It serves as the reference to the single source of truth for all *CF/CE* data and information.
2. The *NPX* is the place where *Producers* update and *Consumers* access *NPC.* It is also the primary source of data to determine potential risks like delivery timelines and personnel overload.
3. An *NPX* can be created using a spreadsheet with column filtering (i.e., Excel), but can also be deployed as a relational database, providing that real-time access by all *Colleagues* is available, as well as the ability to filter and sort on any of the fields or columns.
4. See *NPX* in *Key Artifacts.*

Nexus Point (NP), Nexus Point Content (NPC)

1. A *Nexus Point* is where a piece of data or information (*Content*) needs to be delivered from a *Producer* to one or more *Consumers*, outside the *Producer's Workstream*.

2. *NPs* have a number of required core values associated with them:

    a. The name and description of what is to be delivered.

    b. A single *Producer* who is responsible for delivery. Joint or team Producership, while permitted for the production of the *Content*, is not allowed as a named *Colleague*; an *NP* must have one and only one responsible *Producer*.

    c. A Producer/Consumer negotiated delivery date when the *NPC* will be delivered and available (also known as *Promise Date*).

    d. The actual delivery date.

    e. One or more *Consumers*. It should be obvious, but no active *NPs* should exist without at least 1 *Consumer*.

    f. The *Content* itself or a link to it. Some *NPs* will represent decisions or single items like a yes or no value or a tax ID number. Other *NPs* will consist of individual documents or collections of documents, like a folder of contracts that need to be reviewed during due diligence.

Noise

1. *Noise* in the context of CRISP™ is any unnecessary interruption, diversion, or intrusion into the orderly exchange of mission-critical content required for a successful execution of an M&A initiative.

2. Examples of *Noise* include:

   a. Non-specific Reply-All emails
   b. Instant or direct messaging requests for predictably required *CF/CE* information.
   c. Unplanned drop-bys or calls looking for information.
   d. Regularly scheduled meetings without agendas or goals.
   e. Most requests for interim deliverable status.
   f. See *Hierarchical Filtering*

3. CRISP™ seeks to reduce or eliminate *Consumer* and supervisor *Noise* coming from instant/direct messaging, email, phone calls, and sometimes physical visits and directed at *Producers*. Why? While these communication mechanisms are very useful for ad hoc generalized questions or emergencies, they are inefficient and error-prone for conveying data that has already been vetted and is easily accessible from a single source of truth. Another way to look at this type of *Noise* is that each occurrence potentially creates a new (and either duplicated or inaccurate) source of truth. Plus, these interruptions come at a measurable, non-value-added cost to all involved. (See Neuroscience section).
4. *Noise* can also be triggered by the lack of information or the insertion of inaccurate data, both of which result in activity that can be counterproductive.
   a. Think of an *SME* who needs a piece of data from a *Colleague* but does not know who to ask. Each outreach creates noise for the people they ask.

Party (Parties)

1. *Parties* in the CRISP™ method are those *Entities* that are signatories to the overriding legal agreements (LOI, purchase and sale, transition service).

2. *Parties* in this context do not include consultants, advisors, or any supplier unless specified in the deal documents.

Producer

1. *Producers* have an obligation to participate in CRISP™ *Protocols*, deliver *Nexus Point Content* when promised, and establish content change and notification protocols with their *Consumers* relative to their *NPs*.
2. CRISP™ allows *Producers* to also be *Consumers* when needed, and vice versa.

Protocol

1. A *Protocol* is a code of conduct; rules for how to do things, decision-making frameworks, or how to update a simple glossary. It may include explicit instructions or generalized rules. An example of a general rule included in the *Workstream Protocol* is: "When delivery of *NPC* is late, the *NP* is escalated immediately to the *Workstream Lead* for disposition." Some of you reading this may already have systems that can do this.
2. CRISP™ defined *Protocols* include, but are not limited to: *NPX* maintenance, *TSA* change orders, and various *Key Event* formats (*SteerCo, Workstream Leads*, Alignment, etc.).
3. All *Colleagues* are expected to follow defined *Protocols* wherever they are in force.
4. As necessary, the *IMO* is responsible for enforcing *Protocol* compliance.
5. Protocols are codified in CRISP Tactical Field Guides, which are available under the CRISP license. DIY implementations will need to create their own set of TFG's to guide Colleagues.

Subject Matter Expert (SME)

1. An individual *Colleague* whose specific performance is required in service of the initiative.
2. Executives can be *SMEs* even if their only contribution is a single decision. Likewise, HR or IT analysts are also *SMEs*.

Tactical Field Guide (TFG)

1. A *TFG* is a structured set of instructions that includes *Protocols* and *Key Artifacts* that enable adopting and using CRISP™ in an optimized state.
2. CRISP™ *TFGs* are designed and organized from a practitioner's perspective. This means there is a logical and deliberate ordering of the *TFGs* to minimize time and maximize efficiency.
3. Note: The specific content and structure for *TFGs* are not included in this book. See CRISP™ licensing details for how to access *TFG* content.

Transaction(s)

1. *Transactions* are an overarching term used to describe the agreement to pursue any of the various forms of M&A activity.
2. Included in this mix are spin-offs (internal, single-*Entity Transactions*), carve-outs, divestitures, mergers, and acquisitions.
3. While CRISP™ is optimized to aid those *Transactions* that directly involve people, process, and technology, it can also be used to help manage "paper-only" *Transactions*, where Producership is transferred at the close, but no post-close transitional changes to environments are made.
4. *Initiative* is also used interchangeably with *Transaction*.

Transition Services Agreement (TSA)

1. The *TSA* is a formal contractual agreement, outlining the terms and conditions under which the *Parties* agree to provide certain services for a specified period after the *Transaction* closes. These services are primarily associated with acquisitions or carve-outs and are intended to support the Buyer in maintaining business operations and ensuring a smooth transition during the post-close integration process.
2. For an IMO, the structural design and rendering of the *TSA,* typically done by legal counsel, can have a significant impact on the ease with which a transition can be performed, as well as potential cost recovery for the *Party* providing the service.
3. See *TSA Matrix* in *Key Artifacts.*

3-Click Rule

1. CRISP™ has an aspirational goal of delivering *CF/CE* mission-critical content in three clicks or less using just an instantiation* of the *Nexus Point Exchange (NPX).*
2. Mechanisms/features of a CRISP™ *NPX* allow this goal to be realized >80% of the time, even with complex queries.
3. **NPXs* are designed to be created with a common tool like Excel or Google Sheets, with the ability to filter/search. Nothing more is needed.
4. See *NPX* in *Key Artifacts.*

Workstream

1. A *Workstream* refers to a distinct set of activities or tasks that focus on a specific area of the *Transaction.* CRISP™ allows Parties to

create as many or as few *Workstreams* as are necessary to complete the *Transaction*.

2. Here's a list of common *Workstreams* and their scopes:

Workstream Label	Description
Finance	Manages financial reporting, accounting, budgeting, and compliance issues.
Human Resources	Handles employee integration, benefits alignment, and organizational design.
IT and Systems	Ensures integration of technology systems, data migration, and cybersecurity.
Operations	Focuses on the integration of operational processes and supply chain management.
Sales and Marketing	Aligns sales strategies, marketing campaigns, and customer relationships.
Legal and Compliance	Addresses legal matters, regulatory compliance, and contractual obligations.
Communications	Manages internal and external communications to stakeholders and employees.
Product and Services	Aligns product lines, service offerings, and development roadmaps.
Facilities	Manages physical assets, real estate, and office space consolidation.
Culture and Change Management	Focuses on aligning corporate cultures and managing change initiatives.
Customer Integration	Ensures smooth transition and communication with customers.
Risk Management	Identifies and mitigates risks associated with the integration process.
Supply Chain	Integrates supply chain operations, vendor management, and logistics.
R&D (Research and Development)	Aligns innovation strategies, research projects, and development efforts.
Procurement	Consolidates procurement processes, supplier contracts, and cost synergies.

Workstream Lead (WL)

1. *WLs* ensure the *Producers* within their *Workstream* honor their commitments. This includes accountability for not only delivery dates, but also the quality of the deliverable as well. They are the 1st escalation point when delivery issues arise.

2. *WLs* participate in regularly cadenced sessions with their *Party's* other *WLs* and joint sessions with other *Party's WLs,* which serve as an escalation disposition venue. Depending on how CRISP™ is adopted, they can receive detailed reports on the performance of their *Producers* prior to a *WL* session. Or perform the approved method of referencing the *NPX* on their own to monitor what is being delivered. Either way, visibility into *Producer* commitments is transparent and available for all to see.

3. *WLs* are accountable for communicating initiative-level information to their respective streams. When necessary, this includes reinforcing compliance with CRISP™ *Protocols*.

4. It's worth mentioning that it is not the responsibility of the *IMO* (or similar orgs) to pester, hound, nag, bother, harass, disturb, cajole, or otherwise attempt to influence non-performing *Producers*. The CRISP™ rule covering this behavior is straightforward: delinquent *Producers* are immediately escalated to *Workstream Leads* for disposition, full stop. If *WL* intervention does not produce a timely resolution, escalation to the *SteerCo* comes next, where the context of the issue is openly discussed and a decision is made to rectify the deficiency or acknowledge and accept the risks of taking no action.

Appendix B: The Neuroscience Behind CRISP™

Execution is not just about processes and tools; it is about people. This section connects CRISP™ to findings in neuroscience and psychology. Specifically, why:

- Forced multitasking reduces output quality.
- Messaging and decision fatigue undermine judgment.
- Self-serving behavior is an asset to be leveraged rather than a liability to be avoided.

CRISP™, as a communication-first, deliverable-based approach, is grounded in how the human brain processes information. Modern neuroscience and psychology highlight that traditional management approaches frequently ignore the brain's limits. This oversight leads to cognitive overload, poor decision-making, and declining performance.

CRISP™ reduces noise, preserves attention, and aligns contributors by operating within the natural boundaries of human cognition. This section explores how brain science underpins CRISP™, with structured insights on signal processing, decision-making, multitasking, and self-serving behavior.

Signal Processing: Low Bandwidth and Noise

Human beings have strict biological constraints on how much information they can process. Research by Mihaly Csikszentmihalyi (1990) shows that the maximum information intake is about 120 bits per second. A normal conversation consumes half of that capacity. This means that even modest distractions—background noise, a phone alert, or an unrelated thought—can quickly and materially affect processing channels.

The modern world floods us with 4,000–10,000 branded messages daily (Story, 2014), hundreds of emails, and constant notifications. Earl Miller, a neuroscientist at MIT, notes that humans are "single-channel processors" who suffer major losses when bombarded with parallel streams (Miller, 2009). CRISP™ addresses this reality by filtering communication to reduce noise and ensure that contributors receive only the signals relevant to their deliverables.

Example: A corporate development manager receives 150 emails per day. Most are irrelevant CCs, generic status updates, or noise disguised as urgency. Under CRISP™, instead of parsing every message, the manager sees only deliverable-specific communication, mapped to their role as Producer or Consumer. This preserves scarce bandwidth for critical information.

Daniel Levitin's The Organized Mind (2014) argues that humans offload information into external systems like lists, calendars, and filing systems to cope with these bandwidth limits.

Decision Making Under Constraints

Decision-making is metabolically expensive. Each decision consumes glucose and neurotransmitter reserves (Baumeister & Tierney, 2011). As trivial choices accumulate upon waking, individuals experience decision fatigue, resulting in poorer judgment later in the day. Roy Baumeister's experiments demonstrate that subjects forced to make repeated minor decisions show less self-control in subsequent tasks. Kahneman's Thinking, Fast and Slow (2011) explains this through the dual-system model: System 1 (fast, intuitive) and System 2 (slow, deliberate). Under fatigue or overload, System 1 dominates, leading to biased, error-prone outcomes.

Memory distortions further complicate decision-making. Elizabeth Loftus (2003) has shown that false memories are easily implanted, and retrieval failures are common even for important events. These imperfections undermine confidence in recall and evidence evaluation. Structured methods like CRISP™ mitigate these issues by externalizing memory and embedding routine decisions into shared artifacts such as the Nexus Point Exchange and the Request List. This reduces the burden on individual cognition, freeing contributors to focus on judgment where it truly matters.

Example: During M&A integration, executives often face dozens of trivial process choices daily. By standardizing and externalizing these into artifacts, CRISP™ reduces fatigue, enabling them to devote more mental energy to evaluating strategic alignment or cultural risks.

Multitasking: The Price of Interruptions

The myth of multitasking has been thoroughly debunked, but the term continues to have positive connotations. True multitasking is confined to autonomic functions like breathing and heartbeat. What most people call multitasking is actually rapid task-switching, which carries significant costs.

Research at Stanford University (Ophir, Nass, & Wagner, 2009) found that heavy media multitaskers perform worse on attention and memory tasks than light multitaskers. Glenn Wilson (2005) concluded that cognitive losses from frequent task-switching exceed those from marijuana use. Gloria Mark (2008) found that after workplace interruptions, it takes an average of 23 minutes to return to the original task.

Every interruption forces the brain to reset, consuming glucose and depleting neurotransmitters. Novelty-seeking brain biology compounds the problem: the brain releases dopamine when presented with new information, reinforcing compulsive email-checking or notification-scanning (Kleinsmith & Kaplan, 2016). These loops create a cycle of distraction that undermines deep work (Newport, 2016). CRISP™ reduces these costs by structuring ownership and minimizing ad-hoc requests. Contributors work on one deliverable at a time, protected from unnecessary switching.

Example: An HR SME working on a merger initiative is deep into analyzing potential gaps in health coverage. During the analysis, they receive a chat ping about IT systems, an email about HR onboarding, and a calendar invite for finance alignment—all within 15 minutes. Instead of deferring review of these interruptions, they stop their analysis and triage each message as it appears. Depending on the action triggered by the unplanned messages, the cumulative recovery time (back to the analysis task) could easily exceed an hour, even before meaningful progress begins.

Self-Serving Behavior: Why We Default to "Me First"

Human beings are not naturally wired for collective optimization. Evolution favored individuals who maximized personal gain in competitive environments.

Self-serving bias is pervasive: we overestimate our contributions and undervalue those of others (Pronin, Lin, & Ross, 2002). Dopamine pathways reinforce immediate, personal benefits, even when long-term collective outcomes would be superior. Dan Ariely's Predictably Irrational (2008) documents how individuals consistently act in ways that serve their own interests, even when aware of broader organizational goals.

In large initiatives, this bias manifests as contributors prioritizing what helps their function, their career, or their team—even if it harms integration. Traditional project structures rarely expose this behavior and do nothing to resolve it, instead encouraging siloed behavior. CRISP™ addresses the issue by embedding ownership, purpose, and timing into deliverables, aligning individual incentives with initiative outcomes. By making accountability transparent, contributors see that serving their consumers also serves their own success.

Example: An HR leader SME (in this context, a Producer) may resist prioritizing IT access deliverables, as it seems tangential to HR's goals. Under CRISP™, that HR deliverable has explicit Consumers whose success depends on timely access. The transparency of Consumer needs reframes the HR leader's incentive to deliver promptly.

CRISP™ as a Neuroscience-Aligned Solution

Attention is finite, decision-making is fragile, multitasking is costly, and self-serving behavior is natural. CRISP™ is designed with these realities in mind. By conserving attention capital, reducing noise, minimizing multitasking, and aligning incentives, CRISP™ provides a neurobiologically sound approach to initiative execution. Unlike traditional methods that pile on more communication, meetings, and reporting, CRISP™ aligns with the brain's actual operating limits.

References

Ariely, D. (2008). Predictably Irrational. HarperCollins.

Baumeister, R., & Tierney, J. (2011). Willpower: Rediscovering the Greatest Human Strength. Penguin Press.

Csikszentmihalyi, M. (1990). Flow: The Psychology of Optimal Experience. Harper & Row.

Kahneman, D. (2011). Thinking, Fast and Slow. Farrar, Straus and Giroux.

Kleinsmith, A., & Kaplan, F. (2016). Dopamine and Novelty-Seeking Behavior. Neuroscience & Biobehavioral Reviews.

Levitin, D. J. (2014). The Organized Mind. Dutton.

Loftus, E. (2003). Our Changeable Memories: Legal and Practical Implications. Nature Reviews Neuroscience.

Mark, G. (2008). The Cost of Interrupted Work. University of California, Irvine.

Miller, E. K. (2009). The Prefrontal Cortex and Cognitive Control. Nature Reviews Neuroscience.

Newport, C. (2016). Deep Work. Grand Central Publishing.

Ophir, E., Nass, C., & Wagner, A. D. (2009). Cognitive Control in Media Multitaskers. PNAS.

Pronin, E., Lin, D., & Ross, L. (2002). The Bias Blind Spot: Perceptions of Bias in Self Versus Others. Personality and Social Psychology Bulletin.

Story, L. (2014). Anywhere the Eye Can See, It's Likely to See an Ad. The New York Times.

Wilson, G. (2005). Multitasking Study. Gresham College.

Appendix C: Underlying Communication Logic

In 1948, Claude Shannon and Warren Weaver published their groundbreaking work on communication theory. If you are not familiar with it, here's a high-level summary:

Sender: This is the person or device that wants to send a message. Think of it as you talking to a friend.

Encoder: This step translates your thoughts into a format that can be transmitted. When you speak or write, your brain turns your thoughts into words.

Channel: This is the medium through which the message travels. When you're talking, the air carries your voice to your friend's ears.

Noise: These are any distractions or interferences that can distort or block the message. If there's a lot of background noise, your friend might not hear you clearly.

Decoder: This translates the received message back into thoughts. Your friend's brain takes the words they hear or read and interprets them.

Receiver: This is the person or device that gets the message. In this case, your friend is the receiver.

Feedback: After receiving the message, the receiver responds, creating a loop. Your friend might nod, ask a question, or respond verbally, showing that they understood (or didn't understand) what you said.

While there have been minor tweaks to the model over the last 75+ years, and recent emphasis on specific elements (Kahneman's *Noise: A Flaw in Human Judgement*), the base model remains accurate and useful.

CRISP™'s approach is based on concentrating on the aspects of the model that are understandably problematic in the context of any initiative. What follows are expanded descriptions the 3 critical elements that CRISP addresses head-on.:

Noise: Noise is introduced to an initiative in a number of ways, not the least of which is by *hierarchy filtering* and counterproductive historical artifacts and processes. One example is when communication flow is interrupted by the insertion of people between the originator of the message or deliverable (the *Producer*) and the receivers (the *Consumers*). On a practical level, this filtering is typically demonstrated by organizational reporting structures where managers review, edit, and deliver the output of their direct reports. At its worst, this behavior introduces noise through distortion and omission. At its "best," *hierarchy filtering* retards the speed at which messages travel.

Historical artifacts and processes can also interfere with effective messaging by arbitrarily mandating inappropriate (out of context) artifacts and processes be used with no justification other than, "this is how we've always …". In addition to wasting time on non-value-adding activities, this type of noise pulls focus away from critical messaging.

To be fair, not all established artifacts and processes create this problem. But CRISP™ seeks to minimize (or at least identify) their impact and, in doing so, improve the quality and speed of communication.

Encoding/Decoding mismatches: Intuitively (and accurately), the majority of mismatches are cross-functional. Think of different languages.

Finance, HR, IT, and Legal all have functional-specific vocabulary that is used to efficiently communicate within their domains. But no domain works entirely in isolation. And during the execution of a *Transaction*, there is 100% certainty that all domains will need to communicate with other domains. CRISP™ addresses this communication mismatch with a single messaging concept—the *Nexus Point*—used by all *contributors* (*Colleagues*).

Feedback: Feedback signals in traditionally managed initiatives primarily manifest themselves in the form of countless and unconnected one-on-one phone, email, and direct messaging interruptions punctuated by highly duplicative group requirement and status meetings. CRISP™ changes these dynamics, accelerating messaging by redefining how feedback is managed.

By focusing on the signal, specifically the part of the signal most susceptible to noise, *cross-functional/cross-entity* information, CRISP™'s approach virtually eliminates all noise, achieving the best signal-to-noise ratio (SNR).

Here's what this looks like diagrammatically.

https://crispmethod.com/communication-model/?cm_id=omae

Best SNR = ∞ (no noise, perfect clarity)

In **communications messaging**, however, *infinite SNR* is neither possible nor optimal, because:

- **Some "noise" is inevitable** in human and organizational systems—ambiguity, interpretation, timing, and context are all variable.
- **A small amount of noise can be beneficial**, because it triggers clarification and adaptive behavior (e.g., verifying, adjusting tone, or confirming alignment).

- **The practical goal** is to **maximize the ratio of useful, actionable information (signal)** to **unnecessary, confusing, or redundant communication (noise)**.

So, for messaging, like in CRISP™'s context, the "best" SNR is **as high as practicably achievable**, where:

- Messages are **complete, contextually relevant, and timely** (strong signal).
- There are **minimal meetings, email chains, and unstructured chatter** (low noise).
- The receiver can **act without re-clarification** (high clarity).

Put differently:

Ideal SNR in messaging equals enough signal to enable precise execution with no excess clarification loops.

CRISP™ operationalizes this by aligning deliverables through the *Nexus Point Exchange* and *Request List Key Artifacts* so that every message directly supports a deliverable or decision, effectively driving the signal up and the noise down.

In short:

- **Mathematically:** best SNR = ∞
- **Practically (communications):** best SNR = "No unnecessary communication; no missing context."

Appendix D: Seminal Influences on This Book

Wes Hobby—Who Loves 'Ya, Baby

Despite the difference in age, 17 vs ~40, Wes treated me as a peer and trusted confidant. Even though he was a history teacher, by way of military service and a stint as an EMT, he ran the drama department at Westhill High School in Stamford, CT, for many years. Wes was responsible for competing in and winning top awards at the Connecticut State Drama Festival an unprecedented number of times, one of which was Westhill's first time competing. I was privileged to work on that production as part of a four-person team of juniors; the first year Westhill opened, it had no senior class. It turns out that stellar acting, seasoned direction, and a little partial nudity back then were just the edge we upstarts needed to wrest the title from seniors at Staples High School in Westport, whose drama program was supported by Paul Newman. Wes taught me to be bold and decisive, but not before taking a 360-degree look for obstacles and opportunities.

Rich Katz—This Too Shall Pass

Rich was a self-taught electro-mechanical engineer who introduced me to the world of industrial showbiz. When I met him, Rich was the former technical director for one of the most notable industrial show producers of the time, Jim Sant'Andrea. Rich also suffered from leukemia, type 1 diabetes, and, after we became friends, Bell's palsy, which gave him his self-described evil grin. With urine-inducing delivery, Rich's tales of his journey through the healthcare system were a testament to his positive attitude and will, despite continuing obstacles. He died shortly after his 50th birthday.

Admiral Grace Hopper—Dive Deep; Fly High

I had the privilege of interacting with Admiral Hopper on two occasions, where in one instance, she told the story of one of her Navy exams. She recalled that one question asked to describe how five different ships could be refueled in the least amount of time. She explained that her first action was to dive deep into the key aspects of the problem: tank capacity, current fuel levels, and pump performance for each type of ship—destroyer, aircraft carrier, etc. Then she would "fly high" and look at the problem from a distance: She was working with five ships, all with different constraints. I'll skip to the solution: With a little math, she matched the pumps and tanks and connected all five ships together so they could daisy chain the fuel transfer without having to interrupt the process by connecting and disconnecting fuel lines. The evaluator argued that such a configuration would be virtually impossible to do in open water. To which Adm. Hopper replied: "The question didn't say the ships had to be in open water, it just asked how they could be most efficiently refueled." She got full credit on her solution.

Michael Hammer and Jim Champy—Reengineering

Contracting with CSC|Index just prior to and for some time after "Reengineering the Corporation" was published introduced me to the internal operations of a "hot" boutique consultancy, their business model, and client deliverables. My entry point was through the graphics department, working the 2nd shift. This meant that I had access to all active client presentations (like Pepsi and American Express) plus the core reengineering methodology. By developing strong relationships with the firm's key consultants, I eventually moved out of the graphics department and ended up teaching project management fundamentals to consulting teams. This up-close-and-personal look at the operations of a company in the business of ideas provided not only inspiration but practical knowledge of what it takes to deliver thought leadership and be a catalyst for action.

My Practitioners Library

The following authors and their books/writings have provided me with a variety of thinking and approaches to managing people, process, and technology. The list is by no means complete and is in no particular order.

- Allan R. Cohen, et al, *Influence without Authority*
- James Kotter, *Leading Change*; *Buy*In*
- James Ury, *Getting to Yes, Getting Past No*
- Daniel Kahneman, et al, *Thinking Fast and Slow*; *Noise*
- Isaac Asimov, *I, Robot*
- Peter Senge, *The 5th Discipline*
- Ray Kurzweil, *The Age of Spiritual Machines*; *The Singularity is Nearer*
- Gerald Weinberg/Donald Gause, *Are your lights on?*
- Robert Cialdini, *Influence: The Psychology of Persuasion*
- Heifetz, et al, *The Practice of Adaptive Leadership*
- Patrick Lencioni, *5 Dysfunctions of a Team*
- Charles Handy, *Understanding Organizations*

NOTES

APPENDIX E: WHY TRADITIONAL PROJECT DOCUMENTS ARE NOT USED IN CRISP™

Many project environments rely on Charters, RACI matrices, GANTT charts, and explicit dependency mapping to guide work. M&A initiatives operate under different constraints. They are governed by formal legal agreements, executed under compressed timelines, and require precise communication between individuals across functions and entities. CRISP™ was designed for these conditions. As a result, several traditional project documents become duplicative, inefficient, or counterproductive in this context.

This appendix explains why these items do not appear as Key Artifacts and how CRISP™ covers the intent behind each one.

CHARTER

A Charter establishes purpose, authority, scope, and governance for a project. In M&A, these elements already exist within the Letter of Intent, Purchase and Sale Agreement, and Transition Services Agreement. These legal documents define the work, boundaries, constraints, and expectations across the entire Transaction. Reproducing that information in a Charter adds unnecessary administrative work and increases the risk of conflicts between operational documents and binding agreements.

CRISP™ accounts for the underlying needs of a Charter through existing artifacts.

- Purpose, scope, and obligations come directly from the P&S and TSA.
- All active individuals appear in the Colleague Roster.

- Titles, naming conventions, cost tracking, and milestone expectations are captured in the NPX and Milestone Schedule.
- Approval authority is already codified by the legal agreements between the Parties and reflected in NP-level Go or No Go decisions.

Because the Transaction's governing documents already serve as the Charter, a separate Charter adds no value to execution.

RACI Matrix

RACI frameworks clarify roles and responsibilities in process-centric environments. They are time-consuming to create and maintain, and they require oversight structures that add cost without improving execution in an M&A setting.

CRISP™ inherently fulfills the intent of a RACI.

- Producers are responsible for their deliverables.
- Workstream Leads are accountable for Workstream performance.
- Consultation and informational visibility occur organically within Workstreams or by adding Consumers to the relevant NPs.
- The Colleague Roster provides universal transparency into who can access or monitor work.

Because the NPX already represents responsibility, accountability, and visibility at the deliverable level, a RACI matrix becomes redundant.

GANTT Chart

GANTT charts require stable task definitions, precise effort estimates, and dependency mapping. In M&A, these conditions rarely exist. Transactions move quickly, information changes frequently, and the administrative effort required to maintain a task-based plan cannot be justified.

CRISP™ handles timing and sequencing differently.

- Milestone dates appear in the Milestone Schedule.

- Workstream-specific timing is embedded in Producers' NPC delivery commitments.
- Any changes to timing are communicated directly between Producers and Consumers.

This structure maintains synchronization in a way that is natural to the work, without the overhead and brittleness of a GANTT chart.

Dependencies

Dependencies are real and important, but they do not require a separate document. CRISP™ embeds them within Producer-Consumer relationships, where impact is felt most immediately.

The model assumes that every Colleague understands their role, their workload, the time required to complete their work, and the applicable milestone boundaries. When sequencing conflicts arise, Producers and Consumers negotiate adjustments directly, often long before work begins. CRISP™ rules require Producers to notify Consumers of changes and Consumers to initiate renegotiation when their needs shift. This creates a self-maintaining dependency structure that adapts as the Transaction evolves.

Alignment checkpoints in the Key Events reinforce synchronization without creating an additional artifact to manage.

Summary

Traditional project documents originate from task-based project management. M&A initiatives operate under legal agreements that already define scope, authority, constraints, and obligations. CRISP™ leverages these governing documents and focuses on clear, cross-functional and cross-entity communication between the individuals who are performing the work. As a result, Charters, RACI matrices, GANTT charts, and dependency maps are unnecessary layers that slow execution rather than support it.

NOTES

Appendix F: High-level Benefits Summary

Adopting CRISP™ as an execution model delivers a number of benefits.

The chart in this section shows the benefit categories and the CRISP™ economic, time, complexity reduction, and repeatability benefits that one can expect by following the model.

Here's how those benefits are achieved:

1. **Deliverable-Based Execution.** Shifts focus from task management to deliverables, ensuring Producers provide exactly what Consumers need, waste and delays.
2. **Nexus Point Exchange (NPX) for Alignment.** Uses structured Consumer Tags and Impact Scoring to prioritize deliverables and eliminate unnecessary coordination overhead.
3. **Request List for Buyer-Seller Transparency.** Centralizes cross-stream deliverable tracking, reducing redundancy and improving accountability between Workstreams.
4. **Tactical Field Guides/Protocols.** Provide a structured operational model that eliminates ambiguity, ensuring repeatable and efficient execution.
5. **Minimal Noise, Maximum Clarity.** Reduces unnecessary meetings and email chains by aligning information flow with Consumer needs, streamlining execution.
6. **Data Structuring for AI Readiness.** Organizes deliverables and impact data in a structured way, making it easier for AI tools to analyze and optimize integration processes.

7. **Workstream-Agnostic Coordination .** Standardizes information exchange between Buyer, Seller, and Advisors, ensuring no Workstream operates in isolation or misalignment.
8. **Eliminating Rework & Bottlenecks.** Uses Impact Scoring to identify at-risk deliverables early, enabling proactive mitigation and preventing last-minute crises.
9. **Consistent Handoff Between M&A Phases.** Ensures smooth transition from due diligence to execution, reducing lost knowledge and inefficiencies.
10. **Scalable & Repeatable Framework.** Works across deal sizes and industries, reinforcing process discipline while allowing flexibility for unique deal structures.
11. **Use of Existing Technology.** Designed to work within existing tech ecosystem, avoiding costly deployments and integrations while accelerating adoption.

https://crispmethod.com/high-level-benefits-summary/?cm_id=omae

To see if CRISP™ is right for your enterprise, go to the webpage below (or use the QR code) for a free initial viability analysis and report.

https://crispmethod.com/service/ivar?cm_id=HLBv0

www.ingramcontent.com/pod-product-compliance
Lightning Source LLC
LaVergne TN
LVHW051058210926
848486LV00025B/424/J
* 9 7 8 1 9 9 7 6 4 9 2 8 1 *